Waging the War

D0727579

Waging the War of Ideas

JOHN BLUNDELL

Second edition

The Institute of Economic Affairs

Second, expanded edition published in Great Britain in 2003 by
The Institute of Economic Affairs
2 Lord North Street
Westminster
London SW1P 3LB
in association with Profile Books Ltd

First edition published in 2001 by The Institute of Economic Affairs

Many IEA publications are translated into languages other than English or are
reprinted. Permission to translate or to reprint should be sought from the
Director General at the address above.

Typeset in Stone by MacGuru Ltd
info@macguru.org.uk

Printed and bound in Great Britain by Hobbs the Printers

CONTENTS

THE AUTHOR

John Blundell was educated at King's School, Macclesfield, and at the London School of Economics. He headed the Press, Research and Parliamentary Liaison Office at the Federation of Small Businesses from 1977 to 1982, and was a Lambeth Borough councillor from 1978 to 1982. From 1982 to 1993 he lived in the USA where he was, *inter alia*, president of the Institute for Humane Studies (1988–91); president of the Atlas Economic Research Foundation (1987–91); president of the board of the Congressional Schools of Virginia (1988–92); and president of the Charles G. Koch and Claude R. Lambe Charitable Foundations (1991–2).

He assumed his duties as director general of the Institute of Economic Affairs on 1 January 1993.

He also served as co-founder and chairman, from 1993 to 1997, of the Institute for Children, Boston, MA; founder director (1991–3), Institute for Justice, Washington DC; international trustee (1988–93), The Fraser Institute, Vancouver, BC; and founder trustee of Buckeye Institute, Dayton, OH.

He is a director of Fairbridge and of the International Policy Network and chairman of the executive committee of the board of Atlas Economic Research Foundation (USA). He is also a board member of the Institute for Humane Studies at George Mason University, Fairfax, VA; of the Institute of Economic Studies (Europe) in Paris, France; and of the Mont Pélerin Society.

FOREWORD

Basic to the struggle to promote personal liberty is the task of persuading our fellow men not only that free market allocation of goods and services is economically efficient and wealth-enhancing but also, and much more importantly, that market allocation is morally superior to other methods of exchange. *Waging the War of Ideas*, this Institute of Economic Affairs Occasional Paper, containing published papers by its director general, John Blundell, is part of that continuing struggle and duty of liberty-loving people worldwide.

John Blundell's papers and reviews include a short documentation of the war of ideas from the post-World War II days, when communism and economic planning were seen as the wave of the future, to the post-Thatcher/Reagan period. The pro free-market policy of the Thatcher and Reagan administrations went a long way towards laying the groundwork for the collapse of the Soviet Union. As a result of tales of economic incompetence, human suffering and murder in pursuit of the Marxist-Leninist world vision under the USSR's brutal regime, communism no longer has any intellectual respectability. Indeed, save for minor mopping-up operations here and there, communism as an idea has been relegated to the dustbin of history.

The UK's top generals in the war of ideas were Antony Fisher and Professor Friedrich Hayek. Professor Hayek's *The Road to Serfdom*, written in 1944, was the opening salvo of the attack on the ideas of the Fabian Socialists that had taken over thinking in the UK and on the Continent. Entrepreneur Antony Fisher played a vital role in the war of ideas. Fisher's success in the UK's first broiler-chicken farm, mass-producing Buxted Chickens, provided the economic resources that helped promulgate and market Professor Hayek's ideas of spontaneous order and liberty. After all, what is the value of ideas on liberty if they are consigned to dusty library shelves and known by few academics? Unlike many generous donors, Sir Antony Fisher was not passive. He understood the ideas of liberty and was an active soldier in the war of ideas. Moreover, Antony Fisher was key to the start of free-market think tanks in Europe, Africa and the Americas.

Mr Blundell's papers treat us to a thumbnail sketch of the genesis of the Institute of Economic Affairs (IEA). The collection of four photographs hanging in the boardroom of the Institute tells a concise history, as John Blundell explains: 'Hayek advises Fisher; Fisher recruits Harris; Harris meets Seldon. In nine words, that is the start of the IEA.' Thus, in 1956, Ralph Harris (later to become Lord Harris of High Cross) became the IEA's general director. One year later, Ralph Harris was joined by Arthur Seldon who became the Institute's first editorial director. Harris and Seldon co-authored many of the IEA's early papers; the theme then, as well as now, was that market allocation of goods and services, without the heavy hand of government, produces a superior outcome.

During the 1950s and 1960s, when socialism ruled the UK's academic institutions, news media and politicians, the Harris–Seldon publications and those of their colleagues were seen at best as heretical and at worst as fascist. Ultimately, however, the IEA's persistence won the respect of the more thoughtful members of the media and the academic community and also of the Prime Minister, Margaret Thatcher. The IEA's research provided the Prime Minister and her administration with intellectual ammunition to prevent Britain, as Blundell says, from 'becoming the first fourth-world country, namely a rich nation returning to poverty'.

A major shortfall among practitioners of economics is that we have not made our theory and principles readily accessible to the ordinary person untrained in economics. Many of our fellow men therefore fall easy prey to charlatans and quacks, of all political persuasions, promising one version of the 'free lunch' or another. To make economic affairs readily accessible and comprehensible to the ordinary person has been the IEA's stellar forte and this collection of papers by John Blundell is a continuance of that tradition and speciality.

WALTER E. WILLIAMS
John M. Olin Distinguished Professor of Economics
George Mason University, Fairfax, Virginia

As with all IEA publications, this paper represents the views of the author, not those of the Institute (which has no corporate view), its managing trustees, Academic Advisory Council members or senior staff.

Waging the War of Ideas

1 HOW TO MOVE A NATION

(*Reason*, February 1987)

1946: Recently demobilised from Britain's Royal Air Force, highly decorated fighter pilot Antony Fisher finds in the *Reader's Digest* a condensation of F. A. Hayek's classic critique of socialism, *The Road to Serfdom*. It confirms his own worries about his country's tilt toward socialism.

Travelling to London, Fisher seeks out Hayek at the London School of Economics (LSE). 'What can I do? Should I enter politics?' he asks. With Fisher's war record, good looks, gift for speaking, and excellent education, it is no idle question.

'No,' replies Hayek. 'Society's course will be changed only by a change in ideas. First you must reach the intellectuals, the teachers and writers, with reasoned argument. It will be *their* influence on society which will prevail, and the politicians will follow.'

1949: Ralph Harris, a young researcher from the Conservative Party, gives a Saturday afternoon lecture in a small village in southeastern England. Fisher – now a farmer – is present and loves what he hears. Taking Harris aside after the meeting, he explains his ideas for an organisation to make the free-market case to intellectuals. 'One day,' he says, 'when my ship comes in, I'd like to create something which will do for the non-Labour parties what the [socialist] Fabian Society did for the Labour Party.'

Harris is excited. 'If you get any further,' he says, 'I'd like to be considered as the man to run such a group.'

1953–7: In 1953 Fisher starts what is to become the highly profitable Buxted Chicken Co., the first attempt at factory farming in Britain. By September 1954, it is showing a profit, and he can begin to think more about starting a free-market institute.

In November 1955, Fisher and two friends sign a trust deed establishing the Institute of Economic Affairs. Looking for someone to run the IEA, Fisher remembers Harris. They have not communicated since that first meeting in 1949. Harris is now 31 and, after seven years teaching economics at St Andrews University in Scotland, is writing editorials at the *Glasgow Herald*. In June 1956, the intellectual Harris meets the businessman Fisher in London. On the promise of a starting budget of £1,000 and a part-time salary of £10 a week – the same starting salary as Buxted Chicken's general manager – Harris agrees to become the new Institute's general director on 1 January 1957.

Also in the summer of 1956, the embryonic Institute interests economist Arthur Seldon in writing a paper on pensions. A former socialist and the son of a cobbler from London's East End, Seldon had become a classical liberal while studying at the LSE. Within weeks of reaching London, Harris meets Seldon and an extraordinarily fruitful partnership begins.

1987: It is early January and cold. Some thirty years have passed since Ralph Harris – now Lord Harris of High Cross – left Scotland. Today, sitting in the offices of the IEA in London – so close you could hit a cricket ball through Parliament's windows he reviews the list of 250 major corporations that support its work; it has a budget approaching $1 million[1] and a staff of a dozen. For the past decade, its ideas have clearly been in the ascendancy.

---

1   The equivalent of about £610,000 at the the 1987 exchange rate of £1 = $1.64.

Some commentators have gone so far as to call the IEA'S cramped offices the home of the new orthodoxy.

South of London in his home in rural Kent, Arthur Seldon, now 70 but as active, creative and productive as ever, also reviews a list. It is a list of over 300 titles he has produced and more than 500 authors he has nurtured and developed for the IEA. On his coffee table lie copies of the Institute's glossy bimonthly magazine *Economic Affairs* and a new book, *The Unfinished Agenda: Essays on the Political Economy of Government Policy in Honour of Arthur Seldon*, containing chapters by eleven internationally renowned economists including Milton Friedman, F. A. Hayek, James Buchanan and Gordon Tullock.

Six thousand miles west, in downtown San Francisco, Antony Fisher enters the offices of the Atlas Economic Research Foundation, which he established in the 1970s to aid and encourage the formation of new institutes around the world. Now a full-time think-tank entrepreneur, he too has a list – 36 institutes in 18 countries, all based on the IEA model.

On the walls of the former house where IEA has its offices hang the portraits of famous economists, most notably Hayek, Friedman and Ludwig von Mises – but also John Maynard Keynes. And hanging there, too, is Keynes's famous statement that 'The ideas of economists . . . are more powerful than is commonly understood.' It is from here that the IEA team has steered market ideas from total heresy to partial orthodoxy – at least in certain quarters.

Looking back to his decision 30 years ago to give up a secure, well-paid job to risk his future and that of his young family in the service of an unpopular cause, Harris laughs so loudly the tape jumps. 'I was mad!' he says, and one can almost believe him. 'I did not calculate the risk at all! Fisher's enthusiasm and my desire to return to London and do something were sufficient.'

Arthur Seldon was more careful. Becoming part-time editorial director in June 1959, he managed to hold on to his main job as an economist for a brewing-industry association until he too became full-time in July 1961. Ever since his days at the LSE in the mid-to-late 1930s, Seldon had wanted a chance to 'fight back'. This was it.

Government planning was in its ascendancy. Market ideas were scoffed at as old-fashioned – or worse. Recalls Jack Wiseman, a University of York professor long associated with the IEA: 'One day, leaving the London School of Economics, a fellow economist asked if I could use a lift. I said I was going to the IEA. "Good God," he replied, "you aren't one of that fascist lot, are you?" I went to the IEA – he later became Governor of the Bank of England!'

Says Harris, 'We were a scorned, dismissed, heretical minority. There was a preordained path for the state to regulate, to plan and to direct – as in war, so in peace. If you questioned it, it was like swearing in church. At times this overwhelming consensus intimidated us, and we sometimes held back. We often felt like mischievous, naughty little boys.'

It was not at all clear at first exactly what the new Institute would do in the face of such widespread, deep-set hostility. The strategic choices Harris and Fisher faced were limited. British laws governing charitable institutions, as well as Hayek's advice and their own distaste for the political process, ruled out any kind of lobbying and direct involvement with public policy.

One possibility was a broad-based populist organisation. Founder Antony Fisher, who admired the popularising work done by Leonard Read's Foundation for Economic Education (FEE) in the United States, favoured this approach and would regularly send Harris heavily marked copies of FEE publications. Although Harris liked much of what he read there, he felt they were not scholarly enough for the job in the UK.

While Fisher and Harris were debating, Arthur Seldon resolved the question. In the summer of 1957, he handed in a manuscript entitled 'Pensions in a Free Society', which was to become one of the first IEA publications. It was well-reasoned, thorough, non-polemical and of interest to scholars and specialists – but also easily accessible to lay audiences.

Seldon himself believed that market ideas, through education and persuasion, would out-flank the politicians by first winning over the intellectuals and journalists, whom Hayek had once dubbed 'second-hand dealers in ideas'. To this day he uses a military analogy. The IEA would be the artillery firing the shells (ideas). Some would land on target (the intellectuals), while others might miss. But the Institute would never be the infantry engaged in short-term, face-to-face grappling with the enemy. Rather, its artillery barrage would clear the way for others to do the work of the infantry later on. The IEA would show why matters had gone wrong and set out broad principles, while others would argue precisely how matters should be put right. Fisher, whatever his personal preferences, stepped back and let Harris and Seldon run things.

The IEA has from the beginning concentrated on publishing papers and pamphlets for an intellectual audience, works whose sole concern – in the words of the IEA's first brochure – would be 'economic truth' unswayed by current 'political considerations'. The goal of these efforts, the IEA said, was a society in which people would understand free-market economics 'together with an understanding of the moral foundations which govern the acquisition and holding of property, the right of the individual to have access to free competitive markets and the necessity of a secure and honest monetary system'.

An early problem was finding outside authors willing to put pen to paper for the fledgling Institute. 'We were old hat, old-fashioned,' comments Seldon, 'and Ralph and I had to work on everything.' After Seldon's *Pensions* appeared, they collaborated on books about consumer credit and advertising. The latter proved good advertising of its own. When left-wing economist Nikolas Kaldor criticised the book, recalls Seldon, 'This criticism made a very favourable impression in the corporate world. Companies began asking "How can we help?" to which we would say, "Send us a cheque!"'

From the start, Harris and Seldon were adamant that they would always be independent of their financial contributors. This meant not only never seeking nor accepting taxpayers' money but also making sure all donations were 'without strings'. Seldon remembers warning potential corporate donors, 'We shan't say what you want.'

Slowly but surely the IEA began to find an audience. From the start, its books were well reviewed, not by economists, but by journalists in the financial and general news press. The reviewers liked them, says Harris, because 'they were not polemical but well-researched and documented. Facts and figures – not theory – won us acclaim in the early days and led to meetings with editors and journalists.'

But by the early 1960s, economists began to accept the presence of the maverick IEA, and a few even began to suggest titles of papers they might contribute. Founder Antony Fisher wanted to see 'an IEA paper on every topic that might be discussed'. The result was the Hobart Papers, named after the Institute's new address in Hobart Place.

At the time, it was doubtful that the Hobart Papers would find an audience, recalled Norman Macrae of *The Economist* in 1984. 'I remember writing a polite review of Hobart Paper 1 in early 1960, but saying privately that the venture would probably go bust, and that only a fool would write Hobart Paper 2,' he wrote in a pamphlet marking the 100th Hobart Paper. 'This last proved true prophecy, because I proceeded to write Hobart Paper 2 myself.'

The object of Macrae's scepticism – the first Hobart Paper – was Basil Yamey's *Resale Price Maintenance and Shoppers' Choice* (1960). Fisher himself had baulked at the publication of this work. He thought the topic – why manufacturers shouldn't be allowed to require all retailers to sell products at the same price – overwhelmingly dull and unimportant and Yamey's treatment to be far too scholarly. He feared nobody would read it. 'I can remember saying to Ralph, who sent me the draft, that it was so dull, couldn't I have "more fun for my money,"' Fisher says. But Harris and Seldon prevailed.

Yamey's paper was an instant success, going through four editions in five years. One reason, according to Macrae, is that 'it contained the newsworthy – though underestimated – figure that Britons were paying £180 million more a year on price-maintained goods than they would have done in a freely competitive market.'

In fact, this was one of the rare occasions when an IEA publication had an immediate impact directly on policy rather than on the atmosphere or environment of ideas. Edward Heath, a young, rising politician and president of the Board of Trade, seized on the price-maintenance issue and piloted legislation through Parliament in the face of a great deal of hostility, especially from small shopkeepers. At the height of this hostility, he had lunch at the IEA with Yamey, Harris, Seldon and Fisher. Pointing directly at Yamey, he complained, 'You are the cause of all my trouble!'

Throughout the 1960s the IEA grew, adding several new series of titles. The model, later to be adopted around the world, became clear: a flow of well-written, scholarly but accessible studies in applied market economics, released to the press and sold to universities, schools and the general public.

Of equal importance was the IEA's emergence as a focal point, a haven and a meeting place for a growing but still small group of market advocates. 'I remember in the 1960s,' recalls Fisher, 'at one of our poultry industry black-tie dinners, a speaker, a socialist farmer, made a joke at my expense. He said that Antony Fisher was employing the last two economists who believed in free markets.'

But there were more than two, and through the IEA, an informal network of people from academia, the media, the professions and the business world developed. It was somewhat formalised in the late 1960s with the introduction of the monthly Hobart Lunch, where newly published IEA authors would speak briefly about their work. But the network has in many ways remained an unintended, unplanned and informal consequence of the growth of the Institute.

In the early days, both Harris and Seldon had pitched in on all fronts. But as they achieved some measure of success, a division of labour emerged: Harris would raise money, while Seldon concentrated on his authors and their products. Their personalities, says Milton Friedman today, 'fitted together like hand in glove'.

Harris is the PR man, bubbling and bursting with new ideas and suggestions, a salesman able to peddle the ideas and products of the Institute in any forum. Seldon, introverted by contrast, is, in

Friedman's words, 'a perfectionist when it comes to writing, editing and publishing, and an enormously hard worker who over the years is more responsible than any other single person for the consistently high quality of IEA publications'. Says Harris, 'If I'm dressing the window, it is Arthur who is stuffing good things on the shelves.'

In the first half of the 1970s, those shelves began to include an international element. To 'classical' political economy à la Adam Smith, Seldon added publications by Hayek, leader of the Austrian school of economics; Friedman, leader of the Chicago school; and Buchanan and Tullock, leaders of the public-choice, or Virginia, school. Although their approaches differed, Seldon saw them as 'all reinforcing each other and the work of the IEA'.

Of these three schools – all foreign and new to most Britons – Friedman's writings on monetary policy clearly had the greatest immediate impact, coming as they did at a time of high inflation. 'At the last general election,' wrote influential Conservative intellectual Jock Bruce-Gardyne in a 1978 article on the IEA, 'I was confronted by a young working farmer who intervened in an argument over incomes policy at a village election meeting to say that this was all nonsense: we were suffering from inflation because we had failed to control the money supply. He had seen Prof. Friedman on television, as had many millions of others, and been deeply impressed. It was the IEA which had brought the "wizard of Chicago" to this country for the occasion.' Over the long-term, however, the Austrian view of the market as a process and the Virginia economics of politics are arguably having an even greater influence, as they slowly but steadily permeate British thought.

The early 1970s also saw the first sign that the Institute's work was having an effect on policy. Edward Heath won a come-from-behind victory over socialist Prime Minister Harold Wilson in the 1970 general election – and won on a market platform. But market enthusiasts' high hopes were dashed within eighteen months. Heath made a series of critical U-turns and began to inflate the currency, bail out faltering industries, control prices and wages, and generally expand the role of government.

In retrospect, however, the 1970s must be viewed as the IEA's finest hour. Leading an established, maturing, and increasingly well-known organisation, Harris and Seldon launched a barrage of timely, high-quality work. Inflation, recession and the clear failure of big government were the background as Seldon's shells began to reach their targets, littering the landscape with shattered collectivist concepts and exploded myths, blowing apart the postwar consensus.

In 1975, the *Sunday Telegraph* called the IEA the centre of useful economic activity. In 1976, the *Times* said it had become the source of 'a good deal of the most influential economic thinking'. And in 1977, the *Financial Times* wrote that it was the organisation to have most influenced 'public economic understanding'. Warned *Labour Weekly*: 'They are the new orthodoxy and the Labour Government is by no means immune from them.'

In this intellectual atmosphere, dominated by the IEA's micro-studies and macrocritiques, the opposition Conservative Party began a radical reexamination of its roots. With Margaret Thatcher as its new leader, the result was another victorious pro-market election platform in 1979. This time, however, the platform didn't collapse.

Thatcher wrote to Fisher crediting the IEA with 'creating the climate of opinion which made our victory possible' and rewarded Harris with a seat in the House of Lords. Impishly, Harris took it not as a Conservative but rather as an independent, or 'cross-bencher'. Within two years, he had established an all-party group of lords called the Repeal Group, dedicated to getting rid of legislation. Close IEA colleagues openly worry he is now concentrating on the infantry and neglecting the artillery. 'He's spending too much time across the road,' grumbles Seldon.

But Thatcher, he says, 'has done far more than we ever expected'. He points to the reform of trade-union legislation, the denationalisation of many industries, the sale of over a million public-housing units, the spread of privatisation in local government, the cuts in top tax rates, and the abolition of exchange controls, price and wage controls and dividend and credit controls.

Success in the Thatcher years has had its own problems. One is the common accusation that Conservative rhetoric has become so 'IEA-ish' that Harris and Seldon must be, in Harris's words, the 'puppet masters'. However, they have rightly been careful to keep their distance and to point out that government actions diverge from and conflict with their market analysis in many important respects. 'The government keeps sidling up to us,' notes Harris, 'but we keep digging a trench between them and us, and we keep on with our message.'

He and Seldon are also quick to point to many failures and enduring problems. 'We have made no progress at all on the welfare front – health, social security, education, and much of housing. That whole sector seems to be so far wholly immune to intellectual criticism,' says Harris. He believes, however, that 'you can show people that a "free" good is a pig in the poke, a swindle. In the long run we cannot lose on welfare. Education and health keep costing more and more but they can't buy off the trouble. So much emotion is tied up in all of this that it will be a bitter, bloody battle – but it will yield.'

Even so, there will always be a need for the IEA 'because there will always be backsliding and counterproposals from the other side. There will always be tension and a job for market liberals to do.'

After 30 years, Harris and Seldon can see their work permeating all of Britain's political parties and much of academia. 'Even the Labour Party,' says Seldon, who believes it will never regain power, 'has accepted that here is a body of work with which it has to deal.' He feels that the Conservative Party is still divided between those who think 'the government should run all sorts of things' and those who have accepted and embraced markets. Where this latter group has not implemented market reforms 'it is for reasons they should have foreseen, such as bureaucratic and special-interest opposition,' Seldon says. In the future, he sees alternating governments of Whiggish Conservatives and the Social Democratic/Liberal Party Alliance. And within the latter, this old liberal smiles and says, 'Our ideas are percolating very nicely.'

The fundamental change has been one of atmosphere. 'Markets are no longer old-fashioned,' says Seldon, 'and people in the media now ask the right questions such as, "why is [natural] gas being privatised without the deregulation to make it competitive?" That change is far more basic than the fact that Mrs Thatcher has done a few things.'

What is on the IEA's list for the near future? Seldon lists five major targets for bombardment: transport, where he wants to see studies of rail denationalisation; fuel, specifically proposals to denationalise the coal mines; health and education, which account for a high proportion of both government expenditures and employees; and, finally, local government, which he views as 'inefficient, mismanaged and corrupt'.

'If we tackle these five,' he says, 'we will be much nearer to lower taxes, more choice, the decentralisation of power and smaller government.'

To what can one attribute the success of the Institute? First, there is the continuity of its work: 'their hewing to a straight line of principle, without seeking to compromise in order to court short-run popularity,' as Milton Friedman put it to me recently. But the Institute has not been a narrow, dogmatic church. Virginians, Austrians, Chicagoites and market economists of no particular school (and even critics and sceptics who agonise over possible hygiene problems if garbage collection is privatised) all rub shoulders under the Institute's aegis. The IEA's success, says Chicago economist George Stigler, is 'due in good part to its enlistment of many competent scholars without regard for some rigid orthodoxy'.

Second, there is the continuity of its staff – not just of the principals, Harris and Seldon, but of their team as a whole: their assistant Joan Culverwell (January 1959 until recently); publications manager Michael Solly (May 1959 to date); John Wood (in various capacities throughout); and librarian Ken Smith (1969 to date).

Third, there has been the hand-in-glove Harris–Seldon partnership itself. Looking, as one newspaper has described them, 'more like a pair of country solicitors than seasoned revolutionaries', their hallmarks have been politeness and courtesy, energy and enthusiasm, and optimism and fun.

Fourth, there is the Institute's location in the national capital of a small, highly centralised society. 'We should have to imagine New York, Boston, Washington, Chicago, New Orleans, Los Angeles, San Francisco rolled into one to create some United States analogue to London,' James Buchanan and Gordon Tullock once wrote in explaining the IEA's success.

Finally, the IEA has not fallen into the Fabian Society trap of dealing with only one party. Harris comes from a strongly Conservative background but now sits in the House of Lords as an independent. Seldon was initially socialist and then with the Liberal Party; some years ago he calculated that 20 per cent of 'his' authors had broadly left-of-centre sympathies. His strategic placing of the Institute has clearly been of critical importance.

As the IEA enters its fourth decade, it is conducting a major reappraisal of its past successes and failures, its current position and its future. After twenty years on the wrong side of the wall, the past decade has seen the institution and its authors come in from the cold. Thatcher's Britain has been a little heady for market economists. So much so, claims Hayek's biographer, William W. Bartley III, of the Hoover Institution, that there is a tendency to overrate politicians' commitment to and understanding of markets. The danger is that this will lull the Institute into thinking its battle is won and therefore lure it into more immediate policy work. The Fabian Society made such a mistake in 1945, and the vacuum it left made the IEA's task easier.

The debate within and around the Institute is critical – not just for the IEA's sake and not just for the sake of Britain's still-floundering economy. The Institute serves not only as an intellectual centre in the UK but also as a role model for fledglings in the worldwide network of such institutes.

At a Hobart Lunch I attended in May, Harris asked the assembled guests for their views on what the Institute's future strategy should be. Three positions emerged, neatly encapsulating the choices confronting the Institute.

The first is that the battle for market ideas has been won, so the Institute should concentrate on directly influencing policy by issuing position papers, giving evidence to parliamentary committees and so on, *à la* the Heritage Foundation in the United States. In Seldon's military analogy, this would be to join the infantry.

The second position is that the battle might be won, but the perpetual war of ideas continues. Consequently, say advocates of this position, the IEA must keep to its proven formula of providing a steady stream of independent, scholarly and timely analysis; it must keep on firing its shells and blowing up the enemy.

The third group agrees with the second but also argues for closer and wider links with academia. Economists may be moving toward a better understanding of markets, but hostility from historians, sociologists and other scholars threatens to undermine the success of market ideas. The IEA should therefore reach out to people in these fields. To advocates of this position, the most important work will always be with the first- and second-hand dealers in ideas – the scholars, intellectuals, and journalists – and never in immediate policy circles.

Whoever wins the strategy debate, the future of the IEA will depend on its people. The team that has made it successful is now retiring. At age 70, Seldon is no longer editorial director but editorial consultant. Harris is soon to step aside. Joan Culverwell has retired. And the ubiquitous John Wood will also step down soon. A colleague of Harris's at Cambridge in the 1940s, a close friend and advisor in the 1950s and 1960s, and the IEA's deputy director in the 1970s, he is today acting editorial director during the search for a replacement for Seldon. Wood and Culverwell, says Milton Friedman, have 'provided the underlying cement that has held the Institute together'.

What road the Institute takes over the next 30 years will depend on the leadership it must find and the strategic direction it takes. Among the close to fifty people I talked with in appraising the IEA, there was a clear streak of pessimism. 'While one may have a deep attachment to the IEA,' commented one London lawyer, 'it's probably best to let it die – it's run its natural course.' Many noted a dilution in its sense of mission and a failure to recruit and hold the next generation of leadership.

And yet, who would have predicted that a chicken farmer and two economists could hatch the radical changes they have? Whatever its future, the IEA has exceeded the wildest expectations of its founders.

Editor's note

In Antony Fisher's personal copy of his book, *The Case for Freedom*, published in 1948, is an inscription from Professor Milton Friedman which reads: 'Few people have ever been able to do so much to translate their ideas into practice. Antony Fisher's persistence and idealism and dedication deserve enormous credit for the conversion of his ideas from heresy to orthodoxy.'

2 WAGING THE WAR OF IDEAS: WHY THERE ARE NO SHORTCUTS

(The Heritage Lectures, no. 254, at the Heritage Foundation, 14 November 1989)

My goal today is to set a broad historical scene and remind us of those who fought in the trenches for freedom in the 1940s, 1950s and 1960s. I will draw on the strategic insights of F. A. Hayek and describe how those insights influenced the intellectual entrepreneurs of the era. Finally, I will draw some general insights and conclusions for the years ahead.

At the end of World War II, classical liberal proponents of the market order were a besieged minority on both sides of the Atlantic.

In the United States, the Great Depression, the New Deal, the war and the ascendancy of Keynesian thought had all but totally undermined the classical liberalism of the Founding Fathers.

In the United Kingdom, government intervention in the economy had reached unprecedented heights. The troops who had at the end of World War I been promised 'a land fit for heroes' had suffered the depression of the 1920s. This time the returning troops were determined not to be 'cheated'. The 'People's War' – so called because so many had been involved – was to become the 'People's Peace': as in war, so in peace, namely, the government would run everything, and in 1945 the Labour Party decisively swept Churchill aside to take power.

It is against this background that I start with the publication in March 1944 of Hayek's *The Road to Serfdom*, a book totally against the tide of the times.

The Road to Serfdom was a powerful attack on socialism and an eloquent plea for a liberal market order. On both sides of the Atlantic it attracted tremendous attention. Within fifteen months it was reprinted five times in the United Kingdom despite wartime priorities, shortages and austerity standards. In the US, following the University of Chicago's edition, a condensed version appeared in *Reader's Digest* and it became a selection of the Book-of-the-Month Club. And in both the UK and the US, social scientists were moved to write not reviews but book-long responses, Wootton in the UK and Finer in the US.[1]

Among the many who were influenced by *The Road to Serfdom*, I single out four people: Harold Luhnow, Leonard Read and F.A. Harper in the US, and Antony Fisher in the UK.

Let us start with Harold Luhnow. In the 1920s and 1930s, Luhnow worked for his uncle William Volker in Volker's Kansas City-based wholesale firm.[2] In 1932, Volker had established the William Volker Fund and in 1944 Luhnow succeeded him as the Fund's president. Luhnow had already been exposed to classical liberal thought through Loren Miller. Miller incidentally was intimately acquainted with such important business intellectuals as Jasper Crane of DuPont, B. E. Hutchinson of Chrysler, Henry Weaver of GE, Pierre Goodrich (the Indianapolis businessman and creator in 1960 of Liberty Fund) and Richard Earhart, founder of the Earhart Foundation.

On reading *The Road to Serfdom*, Luhnow became a thorough-going classical liberal and, as head of the William Volker Fund, was able to contribute financially to the cause of liberalism.

---

1   B. Wootton, *Freedom Under Planning* and H. Finer, *The Road to Reaction.*
2   For more information on Volker, see Herbert Cornuelle's biography, *Mr Anonymous*, Caxton Printers, Caldwell, Idaho, 1951.

In 1945, he met Hayek and was instrumental in bringing him to the University of Chicago soon thereafter. To Luhnow, as well as Read, Harper and Fisher, the key question was: What should we do? What strategy should we adopt to change the course of society?

Hayek's answer can be found in a number of his articles of the time, in particular: 'Historians and the Future of Europe' (1944); 'Opening Address to a Conference at Mont Pélerin' (1947); 'The Intellectuals and Socialism' (1949); 'The Transmission of the Ideals of Economic Freedom' (1951); 'The Dilemma of Specialisation' (1956). All are reprinted in his *Studies in Philosophy, Politics and Economics*.[3]

The key strategic insights from these writings can be summarised as follows:

- Socialism came into ascendancy partly because of the failure of liberalism to be a seemingly relevant, living, inspiring set of ideas. Liberalism needed reviving and toward this end, Hayek viewed his creation in 1947 of the Mont Pélerin Society, an international community of classical liberal scholars and other intellectuals, as a critical first step.
- History plays a major role in the development of people's political philosophy. For Hayek, 'There is scarcely a political ideal or concept which does not involve opinions about a whole series of past events, and there are few historical memories which do not serve as a symbol of some political aim.'[4] Hayek agreed with an insight others had offered – that more people get their economic opinions through the study

---

3   University of Chicago Press, 1967.
4   *Capitalism and the Historians*, Routledge and Kegan Paul, London, 1954

of history than through the study of economics. Hayek's key example in this regard is the German historical school, which promoted the role of the state and was hostile to spontaneous order. To Hayek, it was very much responsible for creating the atmosphere in which Hitler could take power.

- Practical people who concern themselves solely with current day-to-day problems tend to lose sight of, and therefore influence on, the long run. This is because of their lack of idealism. In a paradoxical way the principled, steadfast ideologue has far greater long-term influence than the practical man concerned with the minutiae of today's problems.

- Never become associated with special interests and beware of 'free enterprise' policies that are neither free nor enterprising – or as Arthur Seldon says, 'Beware of giving politicians dangerous toys.'

- Do not go into politics where you will become imprisoned in a slow process whose outcome was already determined decades ago. Instead, look for leverage in the world of ideas as a scholar, intellectual, or intellectual entrepreneur.

- Over the long run, it is a battle of ideas, and it is the intellectual – the journalist, novelist, filmmaker and so on, who translates and transmits the ideas of the scholars to the broader public – who is critically important. He is the filter who decides what we hear, when we hear it, and how we hear it

- Historically – and here I believe Hayek might change his tune a little if he were writing today – a high percentage of the most able market-oriented people have tended not to become intellectuals or scholars but rather businessmen, doctors, engineers and so on. On the other side of the debate, a high percentage of the most able socialists – disgruntled with the course of history – became intellectuals and scholars.

- Finally, I quote the whole of the last paragraph of 'The Intellectuals and Socialism':

> The main lesson which the true liberal must learn from the success of the socialists is that it was their courage to be Utopian which gained them the support of the intellectuals and therefore an influence on public opinion which is daily making possible what only recently seemed utterly remote.

Remember that Hayek was writing in 1949. He goes on:

> Those who have concerned themselves exclusively with what seemed practicable in the existing state of opinion have constantly found that even this has rapidly become politically impossible as the result of changes in a public opinion which they have done nothing to guide. Unless we can make the philosophic foundations of a free society once more a living intellectual issue, and its implementation a task which challenges the ingenuity and imagination of our liveliest minds, the prospects of freedom are indeed dark. But if we can regain that belief in the power of ideas which was the mark of liberalism at its best, the battle is not lost. The intellectual revival of liberalism is already under way in many parts of the world. Will it be in time?[5]

To summarise Hayek's message: Keep liberal thought vibrant and relevant; recognise the importance of history; be principled and steadfast; avoid special interests; eschew politics and instead search for leverage; recognise the critical role of the intellectual; and be Utopian and believe in the power of ideas.

---

5   University of Chicago Law Review, Vol. 16, No. 3, Spring 1949.

This was the advice Hayek gave Luhnow, Read, Harper, Fisher and others. How did they translate that advice into action?

The Volker Fund, with Loren Miller and the strategic insights of Herb Cornuelle – who was later to become vice president of Dole, president of United Brands and president of Dillingham, and to serve on the board of directors of the Institute for Humane Studies (IHS) – pursued a number of strategies:

First, it supported key world-class scholars who at that time could not obtain positions in American universities. The list includes Hayek, Ludwig von Mises and Aaron Director – what a comment on the intellectual climate of the time!

Second, it helped the then small minority of classical liberal scholars to meet, discuss and exchange ideas. Friedman's *Capitalism and Freedom*, Leoni's *Freedom and the Law* and Hayek's *Constitution of Liberty* all evolved from such meetings. One can also clearly trace the origins of both Law and Economics and the Public Choice school to early Volker programs. In the same vein, Volker put up the funds that enabled the North Americans to have such a strong presence at the first Mont Pélerin Society meeting in 1947.

Third, it employed the strategy that IHS was later to adopt from 1961 on, namely to identify talented young people interested in the ideal of a free society; qualify (i.e. get to know and evaluate) that talent; and finally support, nurture and develop that talent.

Fourth, it published the Humane Studies Series of books at a time when classical liberal scholars were spurned by publishers. These books were distributed to almost all North American college and university libraries by the National Book Foundation.

Finally, Volker encouraged the formation of complementary institutions, among them:

- The Intercollegiate Society of Individualists (ISI), later renamed Intercollegiate Studies Institute;
- The Foundation for Economic Education (FEE);
- The Earhart and Relm Foundations, and finally IHS, the Volker Fund's strategic successor on its expiration.

Leonard Read established the Foundation for Economic Education (FEE) in March 1946. Read had been a classical liberal since knowing William Mullendore, Herbert Hoover's executive secretary, in California. His early associates included Brown of GM, Goodrich of BF Goodrich, Henry Hazlitt and the Relm and Earhart Foundations as well as Paul Poirot, William Curtis and Ivan Bierley.

Read carved out an 'educational' route. He had two goals, namely, to recover the classical liberal intellectual tradition and to disseminate that tradition to the layman.

He was remarkably successful. He played a special role in the lives of many people over many years. Indeed, it is safe to say that had it not been for Read and FEE in the 1940s, 1950s and 1960s, those who followed and expanded the efforts on behalf of the free society in the 1970s and 1980s would have faced a much tougher battle.

F. A. 'Baldy' Harper was a professor of economics at Cornell University when he, too, like Luhnow and Read, read *The Road to Serfdom*. He promptly began using it in his classroom teaching at Cornell. I vividly remember talking with his widow, Peg Harper, in the summer of 1983, about the reaction to Baldy's use of *The Road to Serfdom*. She described how one night a trustee of Cornell, who was a friend of Baldy's, came to visit them at their home and asked that Baldy discontinue using *The Road to Serfdom* in the classroom. In the view of the trustees, its message was more than contentious and, after all, Cornell, like so many private universities, received and looked forward to receiving a great deal of government funding.

From that moment on, Baldy no longer considered himself in any way tied to Cornell. He very quickly went to join Leonard Read on the staff of FEE and by the mid-fifties had moved to California to join the senior staff of the William Volker Fund. In 1961, with the Volker Fund due to expire, he made his third move, namely to set up his own shop, to found the Institute for Humane Studies. In this endeavour, he was joined by people formerly associated with Volker such as Leonard P. Liggio, George Resch, Kenneth S. Templeton, Jr. and Dr Neil McLeod; and among his earliest business supporters were R. C. Hoiles, J. Howard Pew, Howard Buffet, William L. Law and Pierre Goodrich.

Initially, the Institute for Humane Studies continued many of Volker's programmes and was involved in conferences, publishing and talent-scouting. IHS inherited Volker's staff, approach and the strategy of Loren Miller and Herb Cornuelle.

As the 1970s ended, other groups emerged to run conferences, and university presses and trade publishers began to take a serious interest in the work of classical liberal scholars. This left IHS free to concentrate on its unique mission of talent scout, and in recent years it has homed in exclusively on identifying, developing and supporting the very best and brightest young people it can find who are (a) market-oriented and (b) intent on a leveraged scholarly, or intellectual, career path.

Our fourth intellectual entrepreneur is Antony Fisher, who came across the condensed version of *The Road to Serfdom* in *Reader's Digest*. A former World War II fighter pilot turned farmer, he sought out Hayek at the London School of Economics.

'What can I do? Should I enter politics?' he asked.

'No,' replied Hayek. 'Society's course will be changed only by a change in ideas. First you must reach the intellectuals, the teachers and writers, with reasoned argument. It will be their influence on society which will prevail, and the politicians will follow.'

For close to ten years, Fisher pondered Hayek's advice. In the late 1940s he travelled to the United States and visited FEE. While he finally selected a different approach, he learned from Baldy Harper of a new agricultural breakthrough, the factory farming of chickens, and, armed with an introduction from Baldy, he travelled to the outskirts of Cornell and 'met my first chicken farmer'.

Within a decade, Fisher was Britain's Frank Perdue.[6] His widow, Dorian, later commented to me, 'He did more to put a chicken in every man's pot than any king or politician ever did', and in 1955 he incorporated the Institute of Economic Affairs in London to make the case for a free economy to the intellectuals.[7]

He hired Ralph Harris and Arthur Seldon – Britain's 'last two economists who believed in free markets', someone joked – and the IEA began to publish a stream of independent studies, written by academics mainly, but couched in layman's language and accessible to all interested people.

Their strategy was to avoid politics, concentrate on the climate of opinion and educate opinion leaders on market alternatives. For twenty years Harris and Seldon persevered, producing scores of well-researched monographs on everything from housing to agriculture, welfare to exchange controls.

6   As a result of his efforts, the price of chicken plummeted.
7   For a detailed, but short, history of the work of London's IEA, see my 'How to Move a Nation,' *Reason,* February 1987, pp. 31–35, reprinted as Chapter 1 of this volume.

By the mid-1970s, it was clear that the consensus was turning away from state planning and toward market solutions, and it was also clear that the IEA was responsible.

Indeed, on becoming Prime Minister in the summer of 1979, Mrs Thatcher wrote to Fisher, 'You created the atmosphere which made our victory possible.' And some years later, in a speech on the occasion of the IEA's 30th anniversary, Mrs Thatcher added, 'May I say how thankful we are to those who joined your great endeavour. They were the few, but they were right, and they saved Britain.'

Starting in the mid-1970s, the IEA model began to be copied around the world, and Fisher found himself in great demand as a consultant to such fledgling groups. By the late 1970s his mailbag was so large that he incorporated the Atlas Economic Research Foundation to be a focal point for intellectual entrepreneurs wishing to establish independent, public policy institutes. Today, Atlas lists some 50-plus institutes in some 30 or more countries that it has helped to establish, develop and mature.

It is against this background that the explosion of interest in market ideas in the 1970s and 1980s must be judged and understood.

Without the cast of characters I have described and many others – John M. Olin, Randy Richardson, Dick Larry, Jeremiah Milbank, Dick Ware, Charles and David Koch, and so on – and without their far-sighted commitment, we would not be here today and we would not be witnessing a world-wide move toward freedom and free markets.

The temptation now is to think the battle of ideas is won and all we need to do is to implement the rolling back of the state. The Fabian Society in the UK made an analogous mistake in 1945. Following Labour's huge victory at the polls that year, its members rushed into government and left a vacuum in the battlefield of ideas. This permitted the IEA to grow in influence unchallenged by a socialist counterpart until the Institute for Public Policy Research was established in 1988.

In a very real sense, the battle of ideas will never be won. However far we travel along the road to a free society there will always be a temptation to backslide and thus there will always be a job for market liberals to do at all levels, from the practical to the scholarly. In particular, we must ensure that liberal thought continues to be relevant and inspiring. Liberal scholars must continually take up challenging, cutting-edge work and strive to be at the forefront of their disciplines. To draw on Hayek again, we must retain 'that belief in the power of ideas which [is] the mark of liberalism at its best'.

In no particular order, let me outline some strategic thoughts for the 1990s. Of course, I am assuming that all currently successful initiatives or programmes continue.

- Practical people who pursue careers in business and the professions and who retain an interest in ideas are rare. However, they do exist, and some are on the side of market liberalism. In achieving change there is clearly an important role for the 'business intellectual'. At IHS we have started with Liberty Fund of Indianapolis a programme of identifying and nurturing a network of such people – i.e. younger business and professional people who are destined for top-flight careers and who share a concern for liberty. It is from their ranks that I see the future Loren Millers, Herb Cornuelles and Randy Richardsons emerging.

- For several decades now it has been fashionable to fund economics. Despite the waste of some several hundred million dollars, possibly one billion dollars, on endowing chairs of free enterprise, we have been winning in economics for some time. We have also done well in law, philosophy and political science, although much remains to be done. History, moral philosophy and literature are a different matter, and while Hayek stresses history I would stress all three as areas that our friends in the foundation world should be demanding we tackle.

- To the extent that it is possible, we must identify the issues of the next century and invest now in generating the people capable of tackling them. Take the excellent people at the Political Economy Research Center (PERC) in Bozeman, Montana. They have done pioneer work in promoting the understanding of the role of markets and property rights in sound environmental stewardship.

  Imagine for a moment that PERC's funding had been many times higher. Imagine that a whole succession of generations of graduate students, numbering say a hundred Ph.Ds, had come out of its programmes to teach, write for the leading newspapers, publish books and so on. Clearly, the current debate on the environment would be different.

- We must never overlook or underestimate the critical role of the filter of the intellectuals, the people who translate and transmit ideas to the general public. Pre eminent among such people are journalists, but one also thinks of the clergy, novelists, cartoonists, filmmakers, editors and publishers.

  Finding, developing and nurturing young people who value liberty and seek such careers is the object of another new IHS programme, directed by Marty Zupan.

However, we must not overlook the potential for our scholars in this area. Once tenured and well on in their disciplines, our scholars should be encouraged to come out of the ivory tower and join in public discourse. They should not do this early in their careers – it will damage their chances of promotion. But at the right time they should be encouraged to follow in the footsteps of Milton Friedman, Robert Nisbet and Michael Novak.

- We must be alert to the danger of allowing the 'free enterprise' tag to be given to policies that while somewhat market-oriented are certainly not free enterprise. A classic here is the growth of contracting out, that is of governments issuing exclusive contracts to firms to do a job previously undertaken by directly employed labour. I have catalogued elsewhere the problems inherent in such a situation.[8]

   Today, I simply want to note that contracting out is not free enterprise. Yet when contracting out runs into problems, free enterprise gets a bad name.

- Finally, I want to reiterate Arthur Seldon's point about giving dangerous toys to politicians.

   Here let me contrast four recent policy developments: denationalisation, contracting out, enterprise zones in the UK and airline deregulation in the US. UK denationalisation and US airline deregulation have both been successful. Enterprise zones and contracting out in the UK are, respectively, a total failure and problematic.

   The two successes were both based on well-researched,

---

8 'Privatisation Is Not Enough,' *Economic Affairs*, April 1983 and 'Privatisation – by Political Process or Consumer Preference?,' *Economic Affairs*, October–November, 1986.

well thought-out papers, articles, and dissertations. For years, if not decades, scholars and other intellectuals had debated and discussed every aspect of both reforms. As early as 1973 in the UK, I can remember articles on and discussion of how we should denationalise through a programme of widespread stock ownership and many of the other techniques of the mid- and late 1980s.[9] These and various other articles paved the way for the reforms of recent years in the UK.

Similar debates took place here in the US on airline deregulation. The result of such rigorous examination was a pair of sound strategies.

Let's contrast this with enterprise zones and contracting out in the UK. Both ideas suddenly appeared on the policy agenda in the late 1970s and both were being implemented within a couple of years. In neither case was there more than derisory discussion of potential problems. The result: a pair of flawed strategies.

The story I have told of men such as Hayek, Luhnow, Read, Harper and Fisher is a story of heroes. Their courage and persistence are inspiring. So too are the patience, foresight and strategic sense of the many other individuals I mentioned. They built a solid base.

As long as we are not duped into believing either that the battle is won, or that we can now employ shortcuts, the future for a society of free and responsible individuals is indeed bright.

---

9   See, for example, *Goodbye to Nationalisation*, edited by Dr Sir Rhodes Boyson, Churchill Press, 1973, and Russell Uwis's chapter, 'Denationalisation' in *1985: An Escape from Orwell's 1984*, edited by Dr Sir Rhodes Boyson, Churchill Press, 1975.

Afterword

Professor Milton Friedman later (on 25 June 1990) wrote to John Blundell commenting on his Heritage Foundation Lecture as follows:

Dear John,

Your lecture at Heritage is splendid. I have only minor quibbles with it. One is that I do not believe you give enough credit to Dick Ware and the Earhart Foundation for their Earhart Fellowship Program which I think was extraordinarily successful in identifying and encouraging promising free enterprise scholars. It is impressive to note how many of the names that Heritage or IHS or Atlas would list among the intellectual supporters of free enterprise were Earhart Fellows. Dick Ware, I believe, deserves most credit for that. You do mention his name but not the program.

My second comment is suggested by your paper and not something that should have been incorporated in it in any way. I have personally been impressed by the extent to which the growing acceptability of free private-market ideas has produced a lowering of the average intellectual quality of those who espouse those ideas. This is inevitable, but I believe it has been fostered by one development that you properly mentioned, namely the creation of free-enterprise chairs of economics. I believe that they are counterproductive. I have so argued over the years to people who have approached me about the desirability of setting them up or requesting names of candidates.

In any event, congratulations for a splendid talk.

Sincerely yours,

Milton

3 NO ANTONY FISHER, NO IEA: THE CASE FOR FREEDOM AFTER 50 YEARS

(*Economic Affairs*, Vol. 18, No. 3, September 1998)

Without Fisher, no IEA; without the IEA and its clones, no Thatcher and quite possibly no Reagan; without Reagan, no Star Wars; without Star Wars, no economic collapse of the Soviet Union. Quite a chain of consequences for a chicken farmer!

Oliver Letwin, *The Times*, 26 May 1994

A brief life

Born in Kensington, London on Monday 28 June 1915, Antony George Anson Fisher came from a background of mine owners, members of parliament, migrants and military men. He was christened Antony for choice, George for his father and Anson for his mother Janet's family, who descended from William Anson of Shugborough in Staffordshire, through Vice Admiral George Anson, First Lord of the Admiralty and later Lord Anson.

At his passing on Saturday 9 July 1988 in San Francisco, California, we could reflect on an incredibly rich and varied life of entrepreneurship, action and influence. Indeed it is the stuff of fiction, the kind of exotic and varied life normally found only in the pages of thick paperback novels stacked high at airports. Let me try a brief summary.

When Antony is but 26 months old his father is killed by a Turkish sniper in Gaza leaving his mother eight months pregnant with his brother Basil. Antony and Basil are raised by their mother who is definitely not the typical English lady of the inter-war era, having been raised in a small remote New Zealand settlement. Following Eton and Cambridge (where both brothers learn to fly with the University Air Squadron), Antony opens one of the world's first car-hire firms and invests in a new prototype sports car. The former prospers, the latter fails and war intervenes.

Antony and Basil join III Squadron and are soon flying Hurricanes in the Battle of Britain. Basil's plane is shot down over Selsey; Basil jumps but his parachute is on fire and he dies. Antony is grounded for his own safety.

In the heat of battle Antony had noticed how many pilots failed to lay off their fire. Raised in the country, Antony knew to fire ahead of a moving target: otherwise by the time the bullets got there the target would be gone. Consequently he now develops a land-based gunnery trainer to teach novice pilots to fire not at the target but rather at where the target will be. Antony receives the AFC for this work and leaves the RAF with the rank of Squadron Leader.

After a brief spell with Close Brothers Antony purchases New Place, a 400-acre farm near Buxted in Sussex.

Meanwhile F. A. Hayek, the Austrian-born arch opponent of Keynes, is on the faculty of LSE. During the war LSE moves to Cambridge and Hayek spends many a night on fire watch on top of King's College. He thinks about the future: Germany is going to lose the war but what will happen then? The People's War – so-called because so many are involved in fighting it – looks set to become the People's Peace: as in war, so in peace – namely, the government will own and run almost everything.

Hayek is appalled at the thought of his adopted country's great liberal heritage being thrown away so casually and thoughtlessly. So he pens *The Road to Serfdom*, a critical attack on socialism and an eloquent plea for a liberal market order. To his total surprise its publication in March 1944 is an incredible success. It is reprinted five times in fifteen months, despite wartime paper shortages, and in April 1945 *Reader's Digest* publishes a condensed version at the very front of the magazine for the only time in its history.

It is this condensed version which catches Fisher's eye. He immediately goes to see Hayek at the LSE. 'What can I do? Should I enter politics?' he asks. 'No,' says Hayek. 'Society's course will be changed only by a change in ideas. First you must reach the intellectuals, the teachers and writers, with reasoned argument. It will be *their* influence on society which will prevail, and the politicians will follow.'

This is hardly a blueprint for action and for the moment Antony is busy with his new farm; he is also writing his first book, *The Case for Freedom* (1948), and is caught up with the struggle to repeal various sections of the 1947 Agriculture Act. This Act gives government the power to confiscate land from farmers suspected of bad husbandry. Antony is appalled and leads a delegation from the Farmers and Smallholders Association to see the agriculture minister Sir Thomas Dugdale. Oliver Smedley and George Winder are close allies in this fight and they declare victory on Thursday 23 July 1954 in an article in the City Press.

In 1949 Antony meets Ralph Harris, Political Education Officer (South East Area) for the Conservative Party. Harris is giving a Saturday afternoon talk in East Grinstead, Sussex. Fisher is in the audience and is impressed. He walks Harris back to the station and talks of his hopes that 'one day, when my ship comes in, I'd like to create something which will do for the non-Labour parties what the Fabian Society did for the Labour Party.' Harris replies: 'If you get any further I'd like to be considered as the man to run such a group.'

Three years later Antony still ponders Hayek's advice. Foot and mouth disease hits his farm in August 1952 and his herd of shorthorn cows is destroyed. No cloven-footed animals are allowed to return to the farm for several months, so in October 1952 Antony decides to visit the USA to look at new farming techniques and to try to find an institute he can copy in the UK. He fails at the latter but on a visit to the Foundation for Economic Education he learns from Dr F. A. 'Baldy' Harper of the idea of factory farming chickens. Antony returns to the UK and his farm becomes Buxted Chicken Company. As a result of his efforts the price of chicken falls to a sixth of what it had been and his second wife Dorian later comments, 'Antony did more to put a chicken in every man's pot than any king or politician ever did'.

Now that Antony's ship has indeed come in, he sets about establishing the Institute of Economic Affairs (IEA). Its first book, *The Free Convertibility of Sterling* by his friend George Winder, comes out in June 1955; on Friday 9 November 1955, Antony, Oliver Smedley and J. S. Harding sign a trust deed to establish the IEA; on Wednesday 5 July 1956 Antony gives Harris lunch at the National Farmers Club, and the IEA opens at Austin Friars on 1 January 1957. Over the next 30 years Antony chairs over a hundred meetings of the trustees, is active raising funds and is in constant correspondence with Harris and his colleague Arthur Seldon over editorial matters.

Throughout the 1950s and 1960s Antony is a tireless campaigner, first unsuccessfully opposing the creation of the Egg Marketing Board and second successfully getting it wound up. In

August 1969 Antony and his partners sell Buxted for £21 million and in October invest heavily in Mariculture, the Cayman Island turtle farm. Mariculture managed to do for turtles what Antony had done for chickens. Unfortunately the environmental movement in the USA is hostile to this product and uses the Endangered Species Act of 1973 effectively to close down the business. Antony refuses to hide behind limited liability and goes to extraordinary lengths to pay off all debts. Not yet sixty, he has made and lost a small fortune.

However, it is about this time that it becomes quite clear that the IEA is having a major impact on thinking in the UK and businessmen around the world begin beating a path to Antony's door asking 'How do we create our own IEA?' Consequently Antony embarks on yet another career as a think-tank entrepreneur. By the late 1970s he lists six 'IEAs' around the world including the Fraser Institute in Vancouver, BC where he works tirelessly with Dr Michael Walker as acting director; the Manhattan Institute in New York which he incorporates with future CIA chief William Casey; and the Pacific Research Institute in San Francisco where he settles with his second wife Dorian, who lives in the same apartment block as Milton and Rose Friedman.

In 1981 he incorporates the Atlas Economic Research Foundation in San Francisco. Its mission is to cover the world with new IEAs. For the remaining seven years of his life he and Dorian do just that. From Brazil to Hong Kong and from Iceland to Venezuela, they build a network of 40 free-market oriented institutes channelling useful know-how and significant sums of start-up money.

The Case for Freedom

This year marks the fiftieth anniversary of Antony's first book, *The Case for Freedom*. While much of it is naturally very dated, four passages resonated strongly with me and fit neatly with the IEA's current research agenda.

> On the few occasions when Governments, by luck or design, have followed the right principles, and have accepted the free market system bounded by legislation based on the moral code, then those communities have prospered. (p. 32)

In 1996 the IEA joined with close to fifty other free-market oriented think tanks to create the Economic Freedom Network. The entrepreneur behind this is the same Dr Michael Walker mentioned above. The Network has just one purpose: to help in the preparation, publication and promotion of an ambitious annual volume, *The Economic Freedom of the World* (EFW).

EFW uses seventeen measures of economic freedom and applies them to 115 countries for the years 1975, 1980, 1985, 1990 and 1995. As well as summary tables, it also carries a two-page profile of each country surveyed, making it a very useful reference book.

How Antony would have revelled in its findings: freedom works! The top quintile of those ranked enjoys per capita GDP (1995 US$) of very nearly $15,000 while the bottom quintile barely tops $2,500. The top is six times more prosperous and getting more prosperous still. The top quintile enjoys +3 per cent per annum growth of real GDP per capita while the bottom quintile suffers –2 per cent (negative 2 per cent) growth.

Countries following Antony's principles are leaping up the rankings. New Zealand, Mauritius and the UK are startling examples while countries not following such principles plummet – Venezuela or Haiti, for example.

If prosperity correlated highly with socialism I would still be for freedom and so would Antony have been. Freedom is a good in and of itself and the fact that freedom happens to bring prosperity in its wake is a happy bonus.

> There is only one way to prevent inflation and that is to have a currency out of the reach of politicians. (p. 61)

During Antony's tenure as chairman of the IEA's Board of Trustees (1957–88) the pound fell to 11 per cent of its value on the day the IEA opened and at its height inflation reached 27 per cent per annum in August 1975. Combating inflation was a dominant theme of the IEA's work in the 1970s, in particular with classic titles such as *The Counter-Revolution in Monetary Theory* by Milton Friedman and *Denationalisation of Money* by F. A. Hayek. More recently other related themes have emerged, from central bank independence (*Central Bank Independence and Monetary Stability* by Otmar Issing) to currency boards (*Do Currency Boards Have a Future?* by Anna Schwartz) and from private money (*Private Money: The Path to Monetary Stability* by Kevin Dowd) to the 'productivity norm' (*Less Than Zero: The Case for a Falling Price Level in a Growing Economy* by George A. Selgin).

> If trade is to be free, why have we to be united – the freeing of trade will do all that is required in the economic field. Unfortunately some of those who talk easily of a United Europe or World, think in terms of a huge area of planned economy. (p. 71)

How right and how omniscient: the fear that we would get the

Europe of Brussels rather than the Europe of Rome expressed so early (in 1948) and so clearly.

Building on Russell Lewis's classic IEA paper *Rome or Brussels . . . ?*, IEA publications in recent years have often focused on the future of Europe, from monetary union and its problems to centralisation and from regulation to constitutional matters. Among many such titles, I single out here Clint Bolick's *European Federalism: Lessons from America*, Brian Hindley and Martin Howe's *Better Off Out? The Benefits or Costs of EU Membership*, Otmar Issing's *Political Union Through Common Money?* and Roland Vaubel's *The Centralisation of Western Europe*.

> Let trade be free and the international frontiers will cease to
> be problems. Trade, exchange of services, creates friends; it
> is controls that breed enemies. Huge amalgamations of
> states offer tempting targets for the wrong type of politician.
> (p. 72)

Trade does make friends and, as Bastiat said, 'When goods can't cross borders, armies will.' Indeed, as Hayek taught us, some of the early words for merchant and trade carried clear connotations of peaceful exploration and building alliances between communities. And, as Arthur Seldon is always keen and quick to point out, every time we trade we are making an agreement with somebody and – in the absence of coercion – both parties walk away better off. What could be better?

So, some fifty years ago, Antony was pointing us toward targets that inspired our work in the past, energise us today and will continue to guide us tomorrow.

4 HAYEK AND THE SECOND-HAND DEALERS IN IDEAS

(Introduction to *The Intellectuals and Socialism*, IEA, Rediscovered Riches no. 4, October 1998)

In April 1945 *Reader's Digest* published the condensed version of Friedrich Hayek's classic work *The Road to Serfdom*. For the first and still the only time in the history of the *Digest*, the condensed book was carried at the front of the magazine rather than the back.

Among the many who read the condensed book was Antony Fisher. In his very early thirties, this former Battle of Britain pilot turned stockbroker turned farmer went to see Hayek at the London School of Economics to discuss his concern over the advance of socialism and collectivism in Britain. Fisher feared that the country for which so many, including his father and brother, had died in two world wars in order that it should remain free was, in fact, becoming less and less free. He saw liberty threatened by the ever-growing power and scope of the state. The purpose of his visit to Hayek, the great architect of the revival of classical liberal ideas, was to ask what could be done about it.

> My central question was what, if anything, could he advise me to do to help get discussion and policy on the right lines . . . Hayek first warned me against wasting time – as I was then tempted – by taking up a political career. He explained his view that the decisive influence in the battle of ideas and policy was wielded by intellectuals whom he characterised as the 'second-hand dealers in ideas'. It was the dominant intellectuals from the Fabians onwards who had tilted the political debate in favour of growing government

intervention with all that followed. If I shared the view that better ideas were not getting a fair hearing, his counsel was that I should join with others in forming a scholarly research organisation to supply intellectuals in universities, schools, journalism and broadcasting with authoritative studies of the economic theory of markets and its application to practical affairs.[1]

Fisher went on to make his fortune by introducing factory farming of chickens on the American model to Britain. His company, Buxted Chickens, changed the diet of his fellow countrymen, and made him rich enough to carry out Hayek's advice. He set up the Institute of Economic Affairs in 1955 with the view that:

> [T]hose carrying on intellectual work must have a considerable impact through newspapers, radio, television and so on, on the thinking of the average individual. *Socialism was spread in this way and it is time we started to reverse the process.*[2]

He thus set himself exactly the task which Hayek had recommended to him in 1945.

Soon after that meeting with Fisher, Hayek expanded on his theory of the influence of intellectuals in an essay entitled 'The Intellectuals and Socialism', first published in the *Chicago Law Review* in 1949 and now republished by the Institute of Economic Affairs.

---

1 Fisher, A., *Must History Repeat Itself?*, Churchill Press, 1974, p. 103, quoted in Cockett, R., *Thinking the Unthinkable*, London, HarperCollins, 1995, pp.123–4.
2 Letter from Antony Fisher to Oliver Smedley, 22 May 1956, quoted in Cockett, R., op. *cit.*, p. 131. Emphasis in original.

According to Hayek, the intellectual is neither an original thinker nor an expert. Indeed he need not even be intelligent. What he does possess is:

- the ability to speak/write on a wide range of subjects; and
- a way of becoming familiar with new ideas earlier than his audience.

Let me attempt to summarise Hayek's insights:

- Pro-market ideas had failed to remain relevant and inspiring, thus opening the door to anti-market forces.
- Peoples' knowledge of history plays a much greater role in the development of their political philosophy than we normally think.[3]
- Practical men and women concerned with the minutiae of today's events tend to lose sight of long-term considerations.
- Be alert to special interests, especially those that, while claiming to be pro-free enterprise in general, always want to make exceptions in their own areas of expertise.
- The outcome of today's politics is already set, so look for leverage for tomorrow as a scholar or intellectual.
- The intellectual is the gatekeeper of ideas.
- The best pro-market people become businessmen, engineers, doctors and so on; the best anti market people become intellectuals and scholars.
- Be Utopian and believe in the power of ideas.

---

3   As Leonard P. Liggio, executive vice president of the Atlas Economic Research Foundation, often says, more people learn their economics from history than from economics.

Hayek's primary example is the period 1850 to 1950 during which socialism was nowhere, at first, a working-class movement. There was always a long-term effort by the intellectuals before the working classes accepted socialism. Indeed all countries that have turned to socialism experienced an earlier phase in which for many years socialist ideas governed the thinking of more active intellectuals. Once you reach this phase, experience suggests, it is just a matter of time before the views of today's intellectuals become tomorrow's politics.

'The Intellectuals and Socialism' was published in 1949 but, apart from one reference in one sentence, there is nothing to say it could not have been written 40 years later, just before Hayek's death. It might have been written 40 years earlier but for the fact that, as a young man, he felt the over-generous instincts of socialism. When Hayek penned his thoughts, socialism seemed triumphant across the world. Anybody of enlightened sensibility regarded themselves as of 'The Left'. To be of 'The Right' was to be morally deformed, foolish, or both.

In Alan Bennett's 1968 play *Forty Years On* the headmaster of Albion House, a minor public school which represents Britain, asks: 'Why is it always the intelligent people who are socialists?'[4] Hayek's answer, which he expressed in his last major work, *The Fatal Conceit*, was that 'intelligent people will tend to overvalue intelligence'. They think that everything worth knowing can be discovered by processes of intellectual examination and 'find it hard to believe that there can exist any useful knowledge that did not originate in deliberate experimentation'. They consequently

---

4   Bennett, A., *Forty Years On*, first performance 31 October 1968. Published London, Faber and Faber, 1969, p. 58.

neglect the 'traditional rules', the 'second endowment' of 'cultural evolution' which, for Hayek, included morals, especially 'our institutions of property, freedom and justice'. They think that any imperfection can be corrected by 'rational coordination' and this leads them 'to be favourably disposed to the central economic planning and control that lie at the heart of socialism'. Thus, whether or not they call themselves socialists, 'the higher we climb up the ladder of intelligence . . . the more likely we are to encounter socialist convictions'.[5]

Only when you start to list all the different groups of intellectuals do you realise how many there are, how their role has grown in modern times, and how dependent we have become on them. The more obvious ones are those who are professionals at conveying a message but are amateurs when it comes to substance. They include the 'journalists, teachers, ministers, lecturers, publicists, radio commentators, writers of fiction, cartoonists and artists'. However we should also note the role of 'professional men and technicians' (p. 11) who are listened to by others with respect on topics outside their competence because of their standing. The intellectuals decide what we hear, in what form we are to hear it and from what angle it is to be presented. They decide who will be heard and who will not be heard. The supremacy and pervasiveness of television as the controlling medium of modern culture makes that even more true of our own day than it was in the 1940s.

There is an alarming sentence in this essay: '[I]n most parts of

5   Hayek, F., *The Fatal Conceit: The Errors of Socialism,* in Bartley, W. W. (ed.), *The Collected Works of Friedrich August Hayek,* London, Routledge, Vol. 1, 1988, pp. 52–4.

the Western World even the most determined opponents of socialism derive from socialist sources their knowledge on most subjects on which they have no first-hand information' (p. 14). Division of knowledge is a part of the division of labour. Knowledge, and its manipulation, are the bulk of much labour now. A majority earns its living in services of myriad sorts rather than in manufacturing or agriculture.

A liberal, or as Hayek would always say, a Whig, cannot disagree with a socialist analysis in a field in which he has no knowledge. The disquieting theme of Hayek's argument is how the fragmentation of knowledge is a tactical boon to socialists. Experts in particular fields often gain 'rents' from state intervention and, while overtly free-market in their outlook elsewhere, are always quick to explain why the market does not work in their area.

This was one of the reasons for establishing the IEA and its 100-plus sister bodies around the world. Hayek also regarded the creation of the Mont Pélerin Society, which first met in 1947, as an opportunity for minds engaged in the fight against socialism to exchange ideas – meaning, by socialism, all those ideas devoted to empowering the state. The threat posed by the forces of coercion to those of voluntary association or spontaneous action is what concerned him.

The struggle has become more difficult as policy makers have become less and less willing to identify themselves explicitly as socialists. A review of a book on socialism which appeared in 1885 began:

> Socialism is the hobby of the day. Platform and study
> resound with the word, and street and debating society
> inscribe it on their banners.[6]

---

6   Review of *Contemporary Socialism* by John Rae, *Charity Organisation Review*, London, Charity Organisation Society, October 1885.

How unlike the home life of our own New Labour! Socialism has become the 's' word, and was not mentioned in the Labour Party's election manifesto.[7]

Socialism survives, however, by transmuting itself into new forms. State-run enterprises are now frowned upon, but the ever-expanding volume of regulation – financial, environmental, health and safety – serves to empower the state by other means.

Part of Hayek's charm is the pull of his sheer geniality. He is generous and mannerly in acknowledging that most socialists have benign intentions. They are blind to the real flaws of their recipes. Typically, Hayek ends with a point in their favour: '[It] was their courage to be Utopian which gained them the support of the intellectuals and therefore an influence on public opinion' (p. 26). Those who concern themselves exclusively with what seems practicable are marginalised by the greater influence of prevailing opinion.

I commend to you Hayek's urge not to seek compromises. We can leave that to the politicians. 'Free trade and freedom of opportunity are ideals which still may arouse the imaginations of large numbers, but a mere "reasonable freedom of trade" or a mere "relaxation of controls" is neither intellectually respectable nor likely to inspire any enthusiasm' (p. 26).

Most of the readers of this paper will be Hayek's 'second-hand dealers in ideas'. Conceit makes us all prone to believe we are original thinkers but Hayek explains that we are mostly transmitters of

---

7   *New Labour: Because Britain Deserves Better*, London, The Labour Party, 1997. On the contrary, the manifesto complained that: 'Our system of government is centralised, inefficient and bureaucratic.'

ideas borrowed from earlier minds (hence second-hand, in a non-pejorative sense). Those scholars who really are the founts of new ideas are far more rare than we all suppose. However, Hayek argues that we, and the world, are governed by ideas and that we can only expand our political and policy horizons by deploying them.

He was supported in this view – and it was probably the only view they shared – by John Maynard Keynes. In 1936 Keynes had concluded his most famous book, *The General Theory of Employment, Interest and Money*, with these ringing words:

> . . . the ideas of economists and political philosophers, both when they are right and when they are wrong, are more powerful than is commonly understood. Indeed the world is ruled by little else. Practical men, who believe themselves to be quite exempt from any intellectual influences, are usually the slaves of some defunct economist . . . Soon or late, it is ideas, not vested interests, which are dangerous for good or evil.[8]

Of course, this was true of no one more than of Keynes himself, whose followers were wreaking havoc with the world's economies long after he had become defunct. But it was also true of Hayek. It was Hayek's great good fortune to live long enough to see his own ideas enter the mainstream of public policy debate. They were not always attributed to him: they were described as Thatcherism, or Adam-Smith liberalism, or neo-conservatism, but he was responsible for their re-emergence, whether credited or not. We received a striking demonstration of this at the IEA in 1996 when we invited

---

8   Keynes, J. M., *The General Theory of Employment, Interest and Money*, London, Macmillan, p. 383.

Donald Brash, the governor of the Reserve Bank of New Zealand, to give the prestigious Annual Hayek Memorial Lecture on the subject of 'New Zealand's Remarkable Reforms'. He admitted that, although 'the New Zealand reforms have a distinctly Hayekian flavour', the architects of them were scarcely aware of Hayek at all, and Brash himself had never read a word of Hayek before being asked to give the lecture.[9]

The IEA can claim some victories in the increasing awareness of classical liberal ideas and ideals. It is hard to measure our influence, yet, if we awaken some young scholar to the possibility that the paradigms or conventions of a discipline may be flawed, we can change the life of that mind forever. If we convince a young journalist he can do more good, and have more fun, by criticising the remnants of our socialist inheritance, we can change that life. If we persuade a young politician he can harass the forces of inertia by tackling privilege and bureaucracy, we change the course of that life too. The IEA continues in its mission to move around the furniture in the minds of intellectuals. That includes you, probably.

---

9 Brash, D. T., *New Zealand's Remarkable Reforms,* Occasional Paper 100, London, Institute of Economic Affairs, 1996, p. 17.

5   THE POWER OF IDEAS

(*Economic Affairs*, Vol. 18, No. 4, December 1998: review of three books[1] on the influence of institutes and ideas)

In his classic essay, *The Intellectuals and Socialism*, F. A. Hayek focuses on the key role of intellectuals as the gatekeepers of ideas and, among other things, he wonders why their obvious source of power has not been the subject of greater study. Fifty years later, many of the institutes Hayek inspired to make the case for a market-based society to those very same gatekeepers are passing important milestones. The IEA, often called the 'grand-daddy' of all institutes, passed 40 last year; the Cato Institute celebrated 20 years of influence on 1 May 1997; and The Heritage Foundation is spending last year, this year and next year celebrating its twenty-fifth anniversary.

Two of the books reviewed here relate directly to that Heritage celebration. The first, *The Power of Ideas: The Heritage Foundation at 25 Years*, is very useful, interesting and a welcome addition to the burgeoning literature on the role and influence of think-tanks.

It is of particular interest to IEA subscribers and readers of *Economic Affairs* because The Heritage Foundation's long-serving President, Dr Edwin J. Feulner Jr, spent time in 1965 on the staff of

---

1   *The Power of Ideas: The Heritage Foundation at 25 Years*, by Lee Edwards, foreword by William E. Simon, introduction by William F. Buckley Jr, Illinois, Jameson Books, Inc., 1997; *The March of Freedom: Modern Classics in Conservative Thought*, by Edwin J. Feulner Jr, Dallas, Spence Publishing, 1998; *Heart of Freedom: A Life – A Love of Liberty*, by William L. Law, Wisconsin, William L. Law, 1997.

the Institute. As the book recounts, it was at the IEA that Feulner learned that the integrity of an institute's research is of crucial importance. Being scrupulous brings with it a cost, but the pay-off is that everyone, from the media to your opposition, has to treat you seriously. 'Ed Feulner', claims the book, 'would bring to Heritage the same scrupulosity and firm belief in the ability of ideas to change minds and the direction of government'.

Author Lee Edwards packs in huge amounts of data and lots of interesting anecdotes and stories. I found only one error: Peter Bauer (Lord Bauer of Market Ward) manages to pick up Lionel Robbins's title and so becomes Lord Bauer of Clare Market. However, Edwards is clearly an uncritical fan of Heritage and the occasional sentence is risible. Thus, in Chapter 3, on the incredible job of producing Heritage's first *Mandate for Leadership*, we learn: 'All agreed from the beginning that policy and personnel had to fit together.' Quite! And later, of the seven contenders for the GOP nomination, namely Reagan, Baker, Connally, Dole, Crane, Anderson and Bush: 'Rarely has a national political party offered so impressive a field of candidates for the nation's highest office.'

In spite of this somewhat uncritical, over-the-top, no-warts approach, it is a very useful book to anyone who wants to understand social change.

The second Heritage-related book is Feulner's *The March of Freedom*. For each of the past twelve Christmases Feulner has chosen and published an important essay by a leading conservative or classical liberal thinker, to which he has added his own introduction. Having been on the receiving end of all of these monographs I can personally testify to their effectiveness – both the choice of essay and the introduction are very well done indeed. They command one's attention; they are studied and they are saved.

Now this volume brings together all twelve essays and introductions with a new short introduction to the whole. And what a cast it is: William F. Buckley Jr, Russell Kirk, F. A. Hayek, Milton Friedman, Frank S. Meyer, Midge Decter, Albert Jay Nock, Whittaker Chambers, Michael Novak, Wilhelm Roepke, Richard M. Weaver and, finally, Ronald W. Reagan.

This volume is a treasure trove, but it is probably not to be read from front to back. Rather it is the sort of volume in which one dips and trawls. Feulner's introductions are definitely not to be overlooked. They are lively, informative and very well written. Indeed they amount to 112 pages on their own (from the shortest on Whittaker Chambers to the longest on Ronald W. Reagan) and even those familiar with many of the classic essays will find the introductions greatly entertaining and interesting.

The final volume, *Heart of Freedom*, does not mention Heritage once but fits neatly with *The Power of Ideas* and *The March of Freedom* because it is one man's account of his discovery of classical liberal ideas: how he came to these ideas, how he put them into practice and how he promoted them. Bill Law tells a charming story, but above all it is a great testimony to Leonard Read and the Foundation for Economic Education which did so much to reach out and educate leaders such as Bill in the principles of a free society. Without people like Bill, groups such as The Heritage Foundation in Washington, DC, and the Institute of Economic Affairs in London would simply not exist.

6 THE RIGHT USE OF IDEAS

(*Daily Telegraph*, 1 March 1999)

Yesterday marked the 25th anniversary of the fall of Edward Heath's government. 'Who rules?' he asked the country. 'The unions!' we replied. More important, it was the moment when the Tory party began to reinvent itself. By the time Margaret Thatcher took over, a year later, the first steps towards rejecting the prevailing orthodoxy had been taken.

In place of neo-Keynesianism, prices and incomes policy, exchange controls and accommodation with the unions, Mrs Thatcher and Keith Joseph had begun to lay the foundations of a policy approach based on a commitment to individual liberty, sound money, trade union reform and market economics. Much of this was unpopular or even judged as politically impossible.

In this process, two think tanks – the Institute of Economic Affairs (IEA) and the Centre for Policy Studies (CPS) – played crucial roles. Their widely acknowledged influence and success spawned scores of similar bodies around the world. To this day there is a steady stream of foreign visitors to their offices asking how they helped to change the course of post-war British history. The question most frequently posed by visitors is: 'What's the secret?'

Regrettably, those charged with reinventing the contemporary Conservative Party do not seem fully to understand the 'secret' either. To be more precise, the Tory leadership does not properly grasp the role of think tanks in relation to the wider processes by which the climate of opinion changes, which in turn permits previously unacceptable policies to be implemented.

This perhaps explains why William Hague is reportedly dissatisfied with the performance of existing think tanks, in particular with their failure to provide him with 'the big idea' that would give his party the direction and intellectual excitement that characterised Mrs Thatcher in opposition. It is said that he is therefore backing plans to set up yet another think tank. Those, like me, who argue in favour of competition cannot complain when it happens in their own backyard. But it is perhaps worth pointing out to Mr Hague that the money and effort behind this endeavour will be wasted unless he has a better understanding of what think tanks actually do.

Their task is not to originate big ideas – either off-the-peg or bespoke – for the benefit of politicians. Rather, it is to apply an existing body of ideas – classical liberal economics in the case of the IEA – to contemporary problems, in order to gain wider understanding of the issues and insights into possible solutions. If they are successful, one consequence will be a change in the wider climate of opinion, which in turn stretches the boundaries of the politically possible.

Thus, it is a mistake to regard the politician as a customer and the think tank as a shop. The think-tanker is more of a middleman than either a producer, or a retailer; if the politician is to get something out of the relationship, he has to realise that he is dealing with a 'work in progress' rather than a 'finished product'. Consequently, whatever he gains by way of intellectual stimulus through discussion and dialogue, further hard graft is needed to turn ideas into a form acceptable to his particular party and the country as a whole.

In the case of Keith Joseph, the dialogue with the IEA and CPS, and with the scholars and intellectuals who supped at their tables, was passionate and intense. If ever a man was on a mission, it was the Keith Joseph of 1974 to 1979. Nor was Mrs Thatcher an idle bystander in this process. Every Friday her political secretary collected items for her reading bag from favoured think tanks. They would be returned with marginal comments, underlining and questions the following Monday morning. As a Left-wing Tory MP recalls: 'Although I was by no means an unqualified supporter, it was the most exciting five years of my political life.'

Today, interest in the IEA's work is as likely – perhaps more likely – to come from the Labour Government as from the shadow cabinet. One has only to look at the Government's initiatives on rescuing failing schools, on Bank of England independence, on road pricing, on foster care reform and on new privatisation measures, to detect the unmistakable influence of IEA authors.

Mr Hague's problem is that, for all his obvious intelligence, charm and decency, he has got the policy-making horse and cart back to front. In deciding what to do and say, he does not begin by identifying a body of ideas or principles on which, with the help of others, he can then build. He appears to begin with the findings of a focus group or with poll data. Other inputs come later. This is a sure recipe for policy incoherence; turning ideas into a form that resonates with the public mood should be the last stage of the process, not the first.

Had Mr Hague's current policymaking process been followed a quarter of a century ago, none of the Tory reforms of the 1980s would have been introduced. Not a single one of the many privatisation initiatives – arguably the most successful of the Tory reforms – enjoyed majority support before the event.

To be sure, in some respects Mr Hague has a more difficult task than Mrs Thatcher. During 1974–9, national failure encouraged many to entertain the ideas of the 'New Right', because the old orthodoxy had so obviously failed. The mood of national failure proved a powerful and reliable ally for the then opposition.

In one respect, however, Mr Hague's task is easier. There is now a greater range of think tanks in Britain, the United States and elsewhere, upon whose work he and his colleagues might draw and with which he might engage in a far more extensive dialogue. For example, Digby Anderson, head of the Social Affairs Unit, has shown awareness that political debate has moved on and that there is a new range of important topics to be addressed – from sentimentality, to the decline in manners, to the erosion of the military ethos. His work finds little echo (yet) in the often pallid pronouncements of front-bench Tory spokesmen.

Throughout America there are now scores of think tanks doing useful work, much of it relevant to the British scene. It would be a full-time job just to sift, summarise and distribute all the available material. Again, there is little sign that the Tory frontbenchers have exploited these riches,

As for the IEA, recently its research agenda has expanded to include private alternatives to the welfare state, the role of property rights in protecting the environment and regulation without the state. Bizarre ideas to some, no doubt, but no more so than the sale of public housing, the privatisation of telephones and the reforms of the labour market were judged to be 25 years ago.

Not much time is left for the Tories to bring their blurred party profile into public focus. An election will probably come the year after next. There is no shortage of ideas, but the Conservatives need a clearer understanding of the form they assume, and to be both bolder and more ruthless in taking advantage of them. Otherwise, come polling day, we may *still* be wondering what they stand for, where their party is going and what they want the country to become.

7 MORE ON THE POWER OF IDEAS

(*Economic Affairs*, Vol. 19, No. 3, September 1999; review of four books[1] on institutes and the direction of government policy)

Commanding Heights is one of those big, broad-brush books which span decades and centuries, and countries and continents effortlessly. If you had read *The Prize: The Quest for Oil, Money and Power* it is the sort of book you would expect from its author, Pulitzer Prize-winner Daniel Yergin.

In the opening pages we start with 'the dispersed knowledge of private decision makers and consumers in the market place' and move rapidly to 'government failure' before settling on 'the greatest sale in the history of the world . . . trillions of dollars of assets' and the importance of ideas.

Let me admit a bias at this point. The desk at which I work every day is where much of it all started. Indeed the former David Howell MP, a Thatcherite minister and now Lord Howell of Guildford, recently came to lunch, pointed at the table in question and said

It was at that table in 1968 that we first became serious

1   *The Commanding Heights: The Battle between Government and the Marketplace That is Remaking the Modern World*, by Daniel Yergin and Joseph Stanislaw, New York, Simon & Schuster, 1998; *Think Tanks Across Nations: A Comparative Approach*, by Diane Stone, Andrew Denham and Mark Garnett, Manchester, Manchester University Press, 1999; *British Think-Tanks and the Climate of Opinion*, by Andrew Denham and Mark Garnett, London, University College London Press, 1998; *Capturing the Political Imagination: Think Tanks and the Policy Process*, by Diane Stone, London, Frank Cass, 1999.

about privatisation. It fizzled in the seventies; caught fire in the eighties and today in the nineties burns brightly around the world.

I learnt from Yergin that David Howell discovered the word 'privatisation' in 1968 in the work of Peter Drucker and deployed it in Britain in his 1969 publication, *A New Style of Government*.

Yergin and Stanislaw, his co-author, set out their aim squarely and simply. 'This, then, is our story, a narrative of individuals, the ideas, the conflicts, and the turning points that have changed the course of economics and the fate of nations over the last half century.'

Do they succeed? The answer is an emphatic yes. But we not only get the big broad picture, from Europe to North America and Asia to South America, but also an enormous amount of fascinating detail.

For example, when the four powers occupied Germany after the Second World War, Hayek's *The Road to Serfdom* was banned at the behest of the Soviet Union. Also Milton Friedman, a then young mathematician, 'eager to find a profession in which he could use mathematics ... aspired to become an insurance actuary'. Fortunately he became interested in economics! And such has been the authors' research that the minor classic but little known Friedman (and George Stigler) piece, *Roofs and Ceilings?*, gets its own paragraph.

This is no purist free-market tract. Indeed the authors share familiar blind spots on the environment and demography, to mention just two. But it is interesting (and heartening) that a major superstar author of the stature of Daniel Yergin publishing with Simon & Schuster finds it worthwhile to write trade bestsellers featuring current/former IEA staff, friends, advisers, fellows and authors such as Peter Bauer, Gary Becker, Peter Berger, James Buchanan, Hernando de Soto, Martin Feldstein, Milton Friedman, Ralph Harris, Friedrich von Hayek, Vaclav Klaus, Ludwig von Mises, Michael Novak, Lionel Robbins, Arthur Seldon, George Stigler, John Templeton, Mario Vargas Llosa, Alan Walters and many others.

The contrast with the other three titles under review could hardly be more stark. Indeed it raises the question of why we use taxpayers' funds on think-tank research that is so mediocre when we have brilliant private sector-driven analysis from Yergin *et al.*

Think Tanks Across Nations: A Comparative Approach is the poorest of the three. The choice of countries included, after the obvious candidates, is bizarre and includes not one chapter on the two parts of the world most teeming with new tanks, namely Central and South America and Central Europe. On the other hand, the comparatively dead area of continental Europe gets three whole chapters for France, Italy and Germany.

The three editors (Stone, Denham and Garnett) also have their own think-tank studies: Denham and Garnett's *British Think-Tanks and the Climate of Opinion* and Stone's *Capturing the Political Imagination*.

Sorting out what we do at the IEA and how it impacts on public opinion and policy is not easy. It's like tossing a stone into a pond and then tracking every single ripple, including the ones that disappear. The Geoffrey Howe who toasted IEA authors Robert Miller and John Wood for their *Exchange Control for Ever?* at a late 1979 party denied any influence on their part on the decision to abolish exchange controls when interviewed fifteen years later by the historian Richard Cockett. Indeed, the failure to attribute credit correctly is such a problem that when I lecture overseas on think-tank management I go out of my way to stress getting the record straight at the time. If you privatise the transit authority, get a letter from the mayor of the day and put it in your permanent archive. If you don't, somebody else will get the credit.

Denham and Garnett make a valiant effort to try to sort out some currents or ripples, but any journalist of standing would have done a better job. Their bigger error, however, is to try to dress up a little bit of recent history with analysis and trend spotting and predictions. While this reviewer is treated in an alarmingly flattering way, being an 'excellent choice . . . ' (p. 108) 'who repeatedly warned against complacency' (p. 111), I apparently arrived 'too late' (p. 111) to halt 'a long-term decline in the Institute's fortunes' (p. 115). The doubling of revenues; the tripling of book sales, the addition of three new units, the creation of a student/teacher/faculty outreach programme; the explosion in our conferences and the addition of our huge lecture programme all seem to count for nought.

Diane Stone's *Capturing the Political Imagination: Think Tanks and the Policy Process* is somewhat less disappointing. Indeed, while a lot was familiar a lot was also new and the book improves with each chapter, peaking with Chapters 8 to 11.

Three things would have helped: some *Reader's Digest*-style fact checking, a very good editor to chop (say) 30 per cent of academic-speak, and a more sceptical mind; whole pages at times seem to be utterly unquestioning secondhand reporting of think-tank materials – even think-tank analyses of their own strengths and weaknesses. The worst example is the naive explanation that an attempt to use a McDonald's-style franchise approach to setting up new tanks failed because of a 'lack of foundation interest in funding'. First, it did attract substantial funding, but second, it failed because institutes are headed by individuals with vision and a clear idea of where they want to go, not by automatons following directions from a head office or reading out of a manual or copying someone else's press release – delete 'Illinois' insert 'Missouri'. The IEA has been cloned over 100 times in over 76 countries now, but only twice has the IEA name been used and in most cases the copying of our operational detail is very minor. No doubt the people involved told Stone, 'Yes, it was a wonderful idea but those mean foundation types just could not get it.' Turning a few more stones over would have helped!

However, there was much to chew on in Stone and I hope she sticks with this research agenda.

Four books about the IEA and its cousins, children and grandchildren is certainly one, if not two, too many. Yergin scores A+, Stone B−, Denham and Garnett D, and Stone, Garnett and Denham only an F.

8   HAYEK, FISHER AND
THE ROAD TO SERFDOM

(Introduction to *Reader's Digest* condensed
version of *The Road to Serfdom*, IEA, Rediscovered
Riches no. 5, November 1999; reissued as IEA,
Occasional Paper 122, October 2001, reprinted
April 2003)[1]

My story begins with a young Englishman named Lionel
Robbins, later Lord Robbins of Clare Market. In 1929, at the age of
only 30, he had been appointed Professor of Economics at the
London School of Economics and Political Science (LSE), a college
of the University of London. He was arguably the greatest English
economist of his generation, and he was fluent in German. This
skill alerted him to the work of a young Austrian economist,
Friedrich Hayek, and he invited his equally young counterpart to
lecture at the LSE. Such was the success of these lectures that
Hayek was appointed Tooke Professor of Economic Science and
Statistics at the LSE in 1931, and became an English citizen long before such status had become a 'passport of convenience'.

In the 1930s John Maynard Keynes was in full flow. He was the
most famous economist in the world, and Hayek was his only real
rival. In 1936 Keynes published his infamous *General Theory of
Employment, Interest and Money*.[2] Hayek was tempted to demolish

---

1   This introduction is based on a speech given by the author on 26 April 1999
    to the 33rd International Workshop 'Books for a Free Society' of the Atlas
    Economic Research Foundation (Fairfax, VA) in Philadelphia, PA.
2   Keynes, J. M., *The General Theory of Employment, Interest and Money*, London,
    Macmillan, 1936.

this nonsense but he held back, for a very simple and very human reason. Two years earlier, a now forgotten Keynesian tract (*A Treatise on Money*)[3] had been ripped apart by Hayek in a two-part journal review. Keynes had shrugged off the attack with a smile, saying as they passed one day in Clare Market: 'Oh, never mind; I no longer believe all that.' Hayek was not about to repeat the demolition job on *The General Theory* in case Keynes decided, at some future point, that he no longer believed in 'all that' either – a decision I heard Hayek regret often in the 1970s.

War came and the LSE was evacuated from central London to Peterhouse College, Cambridge. Typically, Keynes arranged rooms for his intellectual arch-rival Hayek at King's College where Keynes was Bursar and – also typically – Hayek volunteered for fire duty. That is, he offered to spend his nights sitting on the roof of his college watching out for marauding German bombers.

It was while he sat out there at night that he began to wonder about what would happen to his adopted country if and when peace came. It was clear to Hayek that victory held the seeds of its own destruction. The war was called 'the People's War' because – unlike most previous wars – the whole population had fought in one way or another. Even pacifists contributed by working the land to feed the troops. Hayek detected a growing sense of 'As in war, so in peace' – namely that the government would own, plan and control everything. The economic difficulties created by the war would be immense: people would turn to government for a way out. And so, as Hayek penned his great classic, *The Road to Serfdom*, he was moved not only by a love for his adopted country but also by a great fear that national planning, that socialism, that

---

3   Keynes, J. M., *A Treatise on Money*, London, Macmillan, 1930.

the growth of state power and control would, inevitably, lead the UK and the US to fascism, or rather National Socialism.

Antony Fisher, the man who did

So let me talk now about *The Road to Serfdom* and one man in particular who was moved by its lessons to do something. That man is the late Antony George Anson Fisher, or AGAF as we referred to him, and still do.

Fisher came from a family of mine owners, members of parliament, migrants and military men. He was born in 1915 and soon followed by his brother and best friend Basil. His father was killed by a Turkish sniper in 1917. Brought up in South East England by his young widowed mother, an independent New Zealander from Piraki, Akaroa, AGAF attended Eton and Cambridge where he and his brother both learnt to fly in the University Air Squadron. On graduating, Antony's several initiatives included:

- a car rental firm – a success
- a plane rental firm – also a success; and
- the design and manufacture of a cheap sports car called the Deroy – a failure because of a lack of power.

At the start of the war Antony and Basil volunteered for the RAF and were soon flying Hurricanes in III Squadron in the Battle of Britain. One day Basil's plane was hit by German fire. He bailed out over Selsey Bill but his parachute was on fire and both plane and man plummeted to the ground, separately.

A totally devastated Antony was grounded for his own safety, but used his time productively to develop a machine (the Fisher Trainer) to teach trainee pilots to shoot better. He was also an avid reader of *Reader's Digest*. Every copy was devoured, read aloud to his family, heavily underlined and kept in order in his study. His first child Mark recalls a wall of Antony's study lined with row upon row of years – decades even – of copies of *Reader's Digest*.

So how did our fighter pilot Fisher come across our academic Hayek? What follows is the story I have pieced together. Not all parts of it are accepted by all interested parties, but the pieces do fit. So this is my story and I'm sticking to it.

The marriage of true minds

The Road to Serfdom was published in March 1944 and, despite wartime paper shortages, it went through five reprints in the UK in 15 months. In spite of this, owing to wartime paper rationing, the publishers, Routledge, were unable to keep up with demand and Hayek complained that *The Road to Serfdom* had acquired a reputation for being 'that unobtainable book'.[4] It was such an incredible hit that Hayek lost track of the reviews and critics were moved to write whole books attacking him in both the UK and the US. Dr Laurence Hayek, only son of F. A. Hayek, owns his late father's own first edition copy of *The Road to Serfdom* as well as the printers' proof copy with Hayek's corrections. On the inside back cover of the former Hayek began listing the reviews as they came out. The list reads as follows:

Tablet	11/3/44	(Douglas Woodruff)
Sunday Times	12/3	(Harold Hobson one or two sentences)
	9/4	(G. M. Young)

---

4 Quoted in Cockett, R., *Thinking the Unthinkable: Think Tanks and the Economic Counter-Revolution, 1931–1983*, London, Fontana, 1995, p. 85.

Birmingham Post	14/3	(TWH)
Yorkshire Post	29/3	
Financial News	30/3	
Listener	30/3	
Daily Sketch	30/3	(Candidus)
Times Literary Supplement	1/4	
Spectator	31/3	(M. Polanyi)
Irish Times	25/3	
Observer	9/4	(George Orwell)
Manchester Guardian	19/4	(W)

But, as Hayek said to me in 1975, they started coming so fast he lost track and stopped recording them.

In early 1945 the University of Chicago Press published the US edition of *The Road to Serfdom* and, like Routledge in the UK, found themselves unable to meet the demand for copies owing to paper rationing. However, in April 1945 the book finally reached a mass audience when the *Reader's Digest* published its condensed version. (Hayek thought it impossible to condense but always commented on what a great job the *Reader's Digest* editors did.) Whereas the book publishers had been dealing in issues of four or five thousand copies, the *Reader's Digest* had a print-run which was measured in hundreds of thousands. For the first and still the only time, they put the condensed book at the front of the magazine where nobody could miss it – particularly a *Digest* junkie like Fisher.

The *Reader's Digest* appeared while Hayek was on board a ship en route to the USA for a lecture tour which had been arranged to coincide with the US book publication. He arrived to find himself a celebrity:

... I was told all our plans were changed: I would be going
on a nationwide lecture tour beginning at NY Town Hall ...
Imagine my surprise when they drove me there the next day
and there were 3,000 people in the hall, plus a few score
more in adjoining rooms with loudspeakers. There I was,
with this battery of microphones and a veritable sea of
expectant faces .[5]

Now I get to the detective work. That late spring/early summer
of 1945 saw both Hayek and Fisher on the move. Hayek had spent
the whole of the war at Cambridge but now it was safe for the LSE
to return to London. Fisher had spent the war stationed all over
the UK training pilots in gunnery and rising to the rank of
Squadron Leader. He too was on the move to the War Office (now
the Ministry of Defence) in central London, just a ten-minute walk
from the LSE. Laurence Hayek and the LSE both confirm the dates
of Hayek's move, while Fisher's RAF record, recently obtained
from the Ministry of Defence by his elder son Mark, clearly dates
his.

Forty years later both Hayek and Fisher were not overly helpful
about exactly what happened next. Hayek in particular used to
claim he had absolutely *no* recollection *whatsoever* of Fisher ever
coming to him for advice. Fisher on the other hand was always
very clear and very consistent about the dialogue – almost verba-
tim – but not so helpful on exactly how it happened. Here is how I
believe it came about.

Fisher, the *Digest* junkie, is already politically active and is also
worried about the future for his country. The April 1945 edition

---

5   Interview with Hayek in *The Times*, 5 May 1985, quoted in Cockett, *op. cit.*,
     pp. 100–101.

lands on his desk as he is moving to London and, after reading the cover story, he notes on the front that the author is at the University of London. A phone call establishes that the LSE is back in place and, one lunchtime or late one afternoon, Fisher makes the short walk from his office to the LSE and knocks on Hayek's door. Fisher also recalled the physical setting of Hayek's office in minute and accurate detail including its proximity to that of the dreaded Harold Laski. Fisher claimed that after small talk (which neither excelled at) the conversation went like this:

Fisher I share all your worries and concerns as expressed in *The Road to Serfdom* and I'm going to go into politics and put it all right.

Hayek No you're not! Society's course will be changed only by a change in ideas. First you must reach the intellectuals, the teachers and writers, with reasoned argument. It will be *their* influence on society which will prevail, and the politicians will follow.

I have this quote framed above my desk alongside Keynes's famous line: 'The ideas of economists and political philosophers, both when they are right and when they are wrong, are more powerful than is commonly understood. Indeed the world is ruled by little else. Practical men, who believe themselves to be quite exempt from any intellectual influences, are usually the slaves of some defunct economist'.[6]

Finally on this issue, let me quote Fisher's own words of 3 July 1985 when he spoke at a party at the IEA to celebrate its 30th

---

6   Keynes, *The General Theory of Employment, Interest and Money, op. cit.,* p. 383.

birthday. (This would have been the 30th anniversary of the IEA's first book in June 1955 rather than incorporation in November 1955 or the actual opening in 1957.) At that party in July 1985 Fisher said:

> It was quite a day for me when Friedrich Hayek gave me some advice which must be *40 years ago almost to the day* and which completely changed my life. Friedrich got me started . . . and two of the things he said way back are the things which have kept the IEA on course. One is to keep out of politics and the other is to make an intellectual case . . . if you can stick to these rules you keep out of a lot of trouble and apparently do a lot of good.

As I said, 30 years later, on countless occasions, Hayek did not dispute the event or disown the advice, he simply said he could not remember. But it is of course very Hayekian advice and very much in keeping with his classic essay 'The Intellectuals and Socialism', which came out just a few years later and which has just been re-published by the IEA.[7] This was hardly a blueprint for action – 'reach the intellectuals' – and indeed the next decade saw little direct fallout from that conversation, although three American intellectual entrepreneurs who had also sought out Hayek did get the ball rolling in the US.[8]

The road to the IEA

Hayek taught at the LSE, got divorced in Arkansas, remarried, moved to Chicago and wrote *The Constitution of Liberty*.

7   Hayek, F. A., *The Intellectuals and Socialism*, Rediscovered Riches No. 4, London, IEA, 1998.

8   See Blundell, J., *Waging the War of Ideas: Why There are No Shortcuts*, Washington DC: The Heritage Foundation, The Heritage Lectures, No. 254, 1990, reprinted as Chapter 2 of this volume.

Fisher tried stockbroking, became a farmer, wrote a very pre-scient monograph, 'The Case For Freedom',[9] imported the idea of factory-farming of chickens, championed liberty in many different campaigns, visited the US looking for institute models he could copy, published *The Free Convertibility of Sterling* by George Winder,[10] incorporated the Institute of Economic Affairs, hired Ralph Harris and, as he always did, having hired the talent let it rip with a very hands-off approach to management. (When in 1987 he entrusted to me the future of the Atlas Economic Research Foundation, the body dedicated to building new IEAs around the world, he made it very clear that he was there if I wanted his help but that he really did expect me to crack on on my own.)

To begin with, in the late 1950s, it was not at all clear what the IEA would do. The exchange control book by Winder had been short, easily understood and on a fairly narrow but important topic. It had sold out its 2,000 print run very quickly because of Henry Hazlitt's review in *Newsweek*. Unfortunately the printer who had also sold the book for Antony went bankrupt, and the 2,000 names and addresses of the purchasers were lost. But Fisher had visited the Foundation for Economic Education in Irvington-on-Hudson, New York, had been exposed to its magazine *The Free-man* and still adored *Reader's Digest*. Harris had been a party polit-ical man turned academic turned editorial writer, while Arthur Seldon, the first editorial director, had been a research assistant to the famous LSE economist Arnold Plant before becoming chief economist of a brewers' association. Out of this mish-mash of ex-periences – academic, business, political, journalistic – came the

---

9   Fisher, A., *The Case for Freedom*, London, Runnymede Press, undated.

10 Winder, G., *The Free Convertibility of Sterling*, London, The Batchworth Press for the Institute of Economic Afrairs, 1955.

distinctive IEA approach of short monographs containing the very best economics in good, jargon-free English, written by academics (mostly) or quasi-academics, in language accessible to the layman but still of use to the expert.

In the early days it was hard to find authors, hard to raise money and hard to get reviews and sales. At times everybody had to down pens to raise money or quickly pick up pens to co-author a paper. The first clear success of this venture – inspired by *The Road to Serfdom*, advised by Hayek, implemented by Fisher and run by Harris and Seldon – was the repeal of Resale Price Maintenance in 1964, a fantastic reform. It effectively outlawed the prevailing practice by which manufacturers priced goods – they literally stamped the price on the article – and discounting was illegal. There was no such thing as shopping around. This change alienated the small business vote and put the Tories out for six years, but it transformed the UK economy and allowed a nation of shopkeepers to spread their wings. It was clearly heralded by a 1960 IEA study *Resale Price Maintenance and Shoppers' Choice* by Basil Yamey.[11] Other successes followed and the IEA's impetus grew, but what was happening to Hayek and Fisher?

Hayek had moved from Chicago back to Europe, and in December 1974 received the Nobel Prize. He was 75 and his health had not been good. He was also depressed. However the prize (and the big cheque) cheered him up no end.

Fisher had sold the chicken business for millions and had put a large part of his minority share into an experimental turtle farm in the Cayman Islands. Well, the experiment worked brilliantly but

---

11   Yamey, B. S., *Resale Price Maintenance and Shoppers' Choice*, Hobart Paper No. 1, London, IEA, 1960.

the environmentalists closed down his largest market – the US.[12] He refused to hide behind limited liability and used the balance of his fortune to pay off all debts.

1974 – now 30 years after *The Road to Serfdom* – was a big year for Fisher too, because, free from business concerns, he was able to respond to businessmen and others around the world who noted the IEA's growing influence and came to him for advice.

Sowing the seed

So the entrepreneur turned fighter pilot turned gunnery trainer turned stockbroker turned dairy farmer turned chicken pioneer turned turtle saviour became the Johnny Appleseed of the freemarket movement, going all over the world and setting up new IEA-type operations.

First he joined the very young Fraser Institute in Vancouver, BC; quickly moved on to help Greg Lindsay and the Centre for Independent Studies in Australia; hired David Theroux, recently departed from the Cato Institute, to set up the Pacific Research Institute in San Francisco; gave support to the Butler brothers and Madsen Pirie as they founded the Adam Smith Institute in London; and incorporated with William Casey the Manhattan Institute where, as they did so, they sat on movers' boxes in an otherwise empty office.

It took ten years to give birth to Institute No. 1 – the IEA. For all but twenty years it was the only one in the family; in just six years five more were born, and then the fun really started. In 1981 Fisher

---

12   For a full account see Fosdick, P. and S., *Last Chance Lost: Can and Should Farming Save The Green Sea Turtle?*, York, PA, Irvin S. Naylor, 1994.

incorporated the Atlas Economic Research Foundation to be a focal point for institutes and to channel funds to start-ups. By the time of his death in 1988 we listed 30-plus institutes in 20 or so countries. By 1991 we were listing 80 and I now count about 100 in 76 countries.

All of this can be traced back to this young economist, his book, the *Reader's Digest* condensation, and a young RAF officer . . . through the IEA . . . through CIS/PRI/ASI/Manhattan and Fraser . . . to 100 institutes in 76 countries today, who together are literally changing the world.

To illustrate our impact, let me finish with a story from Lord Howell of Guildford, a minister in the 1980s. He came into my office recently and pointed at the big boardroom table where I work every day and which was donated by Antony in the late sixties. Howell said: 'You know, John, it was at that table that we first got serious about privatisation in 1968. The idea fizzled in the 1970s, took off in the 1980s and in the 1990s burns brightly around the world'. I replied: 'Yes, it burns so brightly that last year world-wide privatisation revenues topped $100 billion for the first time.'

So it is quite a story we have to tell and it all begins here with the condensed version of *The Road to Serfdom* and the cartoon version drawn to my attention only recently by Laurence Hayek. Read the condensed version, now published in our 'Rediscovered Riches' series for the first time since its original appearance in the *Reader's Digest*, and wonder on all the changes it led to: all the misery avoided and all the prosperity created.

9 FOREWORD TO *THE REPRESENTATION OF BUSINESS IN ENGLISH LITERATURE*

(IEA, Readings 53, October 2000)

At first glance it might seem a little out of the ordinary for the Institute of Economic Affairs (IEA) to publish a collection of essays on the representation of business in English literature over the past three centuries, however good those essays may be.

However, the mission of the IEA is to broaden public understanding of the functioning of a free economy. Thus a very significant part of its work has to do with understanding the processes by which public opinion evolves and, against such analysis, to consider how the free economy is viewed, why it is so viewed, and how such a view might be improved.

When the IEA's founder, the late Sir Antony G. A. Fisher, met with future Nobel Laureate F. A. Hayek at the London School of Economics and Political Science (LSE) in the summer of 1945[1], Hayek was between *The Road to Serfdom* and *The Intellectuals and Socialism*. The former was his call to arms, the latter his blueprint for change. In that blueprint he lists the types of people he believes

1　See 'Hayek, Fisher and *The Road to Serfdom*', my introduction to the IEA's November 1999 reprint of the Reader's Digest *Condensed Version of The Road to Serfdom*, pp. xi–xix, reprinted as Chapter 8 in this volume. It was at this meeting that Hayek told Fisher '. . . reach the intellectuals, the teachers and writers, with reasoned argument. It will be their influence on society which will prevail and the politicians will follow.'

2　In a letter to Fisher of 5 January 1985 Hayek confirms that this essay 'gives a clear account of what I had then in mind in giving you the advice I did'. Hayek later in that letter claims to have found the essay 'pleasantly good' on his rereading of it.

make up the class of 'intellectuals'.[2] Before doing so, however, he makes these points:

- before you try making such a list yourself 'it is difficult to realise how numerous it is'; try it now yourself before going any further – list all the intellectual professions you can think of;
- the 'scope' for the 'activities' of this 'class' or group constantly increases in modern society; and
- 'how dependent on it (that is, the class of intellectuals) we have become.'

Hayek's list then goes on as follows:

- 'journalists, teachers, ministers, lecturers, publicists, radio commentators, *writers of fiction* [my emphasis], cartoonists, and artists – all of whom may be masters of the technique of conveying ideas but are usually amateurs so far as the substance of what they convey is concerned'; and
- 'many professional men and technicians, such as scientists and doctors, who through their habitual intercourse with the printed word become carriers of new ideas outside their own fields and who, because of their expert knowledge of their own subjects, are listened to with respect on most others'.

To Hayek the term intellectual is not very satisfactory because it does not give a full picture of the size of this group of 'second-hand dealers in ideas'. This lack of a precise term he thinks has deterred serious study of the role of such people. He also attempts his own definition which has always delighted me, ever since I first read it as an undergraduate at the LSE.

In Hayek's view, when someone is performing the intellectual function he or she is *not* an 'original thinker' nor a 'scholar or expert in a particular field'. In performing intellectual work he or she does *not* 'possess special knowledge of anything in particular' and 'need *not* even be particularly intelligent'. What the intellectual does have is 'the wide range of subjects on which he can readily talk and write' and 'a position or habits through which he becomes acquainted with new ideas sooner than those to whom he addresses himself'.

Hayek presents a bleak picture. He is clearly saying that this large class of intellectuals consists of two categories. In the first are the people who are expert at conveying ideas but are complete and utter amateurs when it comes to substance and need not even be particularly intelligent. In the second are people who are the true experts in a particular small area; unfortunately this gives them the standing such that they are listened to with respect in all kinds of other areas well outside their areas of competence.

Hayek often told the story of how he nearly turned down the award of the Nobel Prize for Economic Science in 1974 because he feared the impact on him of being asked to comment on anything and everything under the sun with people hanging on, and possibly acting on, every word. Likewise former world number one ranked golfer David Duval (whose tour nickname is 'the intellectual' because he says he both reads, and understands the ideas behind, the novels of Ayn Rand) was staggered at the range of questions, from astronomy to zoology, put to him while he enjoyed that top spot. Fortunately for both golf and society he was sufficiently intelligent to laugh off such inquiries.

Hayek's point about the intellectual not needing to know too much was brilliantly illustrated in *Don't Quote Me: Hi, My Name Is*

Steven, and I'm A Recovering Talking Head by Dr Steven Gorelick in *The Washington Post* Outlook Section, Sunday, 27 August 2000. Dr Gorelick is special assistant to the president at the City University of New York's Graduate School and University Center and his 'Outlook' piece was condensed from the 21 July issue of the *Chronicle of Higher Education*.

Gorelick is an expert on how communities on the one hand, and news organisations on the other hand, respond to high-profile violent crimes. Over a ten-year period he found that having the Dr title, an academic job and being the kind of person who keeps up with the issues of the day, he experienced 'expertise creep' and was soon commenting on topics far outside his general area of expertise.

His moment of truth came when he was asked, 'Should adopted children be encouraged to locate their birth parents?' He framed a suitable response in his mind: 'It is probably not possible for an adult to form a complete, integrated personality without knowing fundamental facts about his or her personal history.' Suddenly he realised he 'knew absolutely nothing about adoption'. He declined to comment and ever since has taken 'the pledge' under which he refuses to be given a platform as an expert on something he knows nothing about. One would think this would be easy. Why would people want your view on something you know nothing about? He reports it is hard as the telephone rings with requests for his views on euthanasia, socialisation and military readiness.

In the Hayekian vision of change there are experts and original thinkers or scholars, that is, firsthand dealers in ideas. But we are 'almost all ordinary men' outside our specialist fields and thus terribly dependent on the class of intellectuals or secondhand dealers in ideas, including novelists, for access to the ideas and work of the experts. The intellectuals truly are the gatekeepers of ideas 'who decide what views and opinions are to reach us, which facts are important enough to be told to us, and in what form and from what angle they are to be presented. Whether we shall ever learn of the results of the work of the expert and the original thinker depends mainly on their decision.'

Time and again IEA authors have turned to the theme of what makes public opinion from *Not from Benevolence: Twenty years of economic dissent*[3] to *The Emerging Consensus? Essays on the interplay between ideas, interests and circumstances in the first 25 years of the IEA*;[4] and from *Ideas, Interests and Consequences*[5] to *British Economic Opinion: A Survey of A Thousand Economists.*[6] A recent Liberty Fund video, in its 'Intellectual Portrait' series, in which Lord Harris and Dr Arthur Seldon are interviewed about the IEA's influence on opinion,[7] is in the same tradition, and, as this Readings concerns itself with 'writers of fiction', mention must also be made of Michael Jefferson's chapter, 'Industrialisation and Poverty: In Fact and Fiction' in *The Long Debate on Poverty.*[8]

In the chapters that follow one is faced with a rather damning picture of prodigiously wasteful, yet Scrooge-like businessmen who are abnormal and antagonistic; corrupt, cunning and cynical; dishonest, disorderly, doltish, dumb and duplicitous; inhumane, insensitive and irresponsible; ruthless; unethical and unprincipled; and villainous to boot. Direct data, loved by economists, are

---

3   Hobart Paperback 10, Institute of Economic Affairs, 1977, 2nd Impression 1977.
4   Hobart Paperback 14, Institute of Economic Affairs, 1981.
5   Readings 30, Institute of Economic Affairs, 1989.
6   Research Monograph 45, Institute of Economic Affairs. 1990.
7   Published in *A Conversation with Harris and Seldon*, IEA, Occasional Paper 116, 2001. See also Chapter 10 of this volume.
8   Readings 9, Institute of Economic Affairs, 1972. 2nd Edition 1974.

not available, but in the closely related field of TV entertainment some relief is to hand.[9] The Washington DC-based Media Institute tracked the portrayal of businessmen in 200 episodes of 50 prime time TV programmes. It found that:

- 'Over half of all corporate chiefs on television commit illegal acts ranging from fraud to murder.'
- '45 per cent of all business activities on television are portrayed as illegal.'
- 'Only 3 per cent of television businessmen engage in socially or economically productive behavior.'
- 'Hard work is usually ridiculed on television as 'workaholism' that inevitably leads to strained personal relationships.'[10]

Put another way, 97 per cent of business is either illegal (Crooks) or duplicitous (Conmen) or foolish (Clowns) and those who practise it have rotten marriages and unhappy kids. . . of course they would have because they are all emotionally atrophied. Would the data for our novelists be any different? I doubt it.

The only possible TV bright spot is small business. Here the protagonist is not so much a vicious, corrupt, murdering drug dealer masquerading as a city banker, as a dumb, inept, social climber, way out of his league and subject to ridicule. So it is not much of a bright spot.

And in *The Businessman in American Literature* (University of Georgia Press, 1982), Emily Stipes Watts lights on a similar vein,

---

9   Hayek was of course writing at the very dawn of television and were he writing today he would surely have included this medium.
10 *Crooks, Conmen and Clowns: Businessmen in TV Entertainment*, The Media Institute, 1981.

namely 'small, private businessmen' but even then openly admits that 'four sympathetic protagonists . . . created by three important post-1945 novelists do not compose a dominant trend' (p. 149). Indeed, less than twenty years later, my US bookstore could not find one of the four titles and was unsure of another.

In some fields of literature, the portrayal of business is more positive. Popular writers such as Nevil Shute and Dick Francis between them populate some threescore or more high selling books with lots of self employed small business characters who are heroic yet humble; problem-solving and law-abiding; self reliant and self interested but not selfish. Long running British soap operas such as *Coronation Street* and *Eastenders* have their fair share of used car dealers of all types but many of the main characters are utterly respectable smaller business people making wonderful contributions to all the lives around them. It is when one moves to a *Dallas* or to a Booker prize candidate that the picture changes and it is difficult, nay impossible, to point to 'literary capitalism' while 'literary socialism' abounds.

So why is the picture so bleak? Why does the novelist, the writer of fiction, spit at the market, despise its institutions such as private property and the rule of law, and try to bite off the hand that feeds him? Surely Hayek again has part, at least, of the answer for us, when later in *The Intellectuals and Socialism* he discusses the role of disaffection.

For Hayek, the talented person who accepts our prevailing current norms and institutions faces a wide range of good career paths. However, to those who are 'disaffected and dissatisfied' with the current order 'an intellectual career is the most promising path to both influence and the power to contribute to the achievement of his ideals.'

But Hayek goes further. The top class person not 'disaffected and dissatisfied' is more likely to opt for the scholarly rather than intellectual path whereas his equally able peer who is out to change things will see an intellectual rather than scholarly route as 'a means rather than an end, a path to exactly that kind of wide influence which the professional intellectual exercises'.

Hayek concludes this section by asserting that there is no greater propensity to what he calls socialism among the more intelligent in society than to any other 'ism'. If one gets that impression from the pulpit or in the classroom or from the television or in novels then it is simply because 'among the best minds' there is a higher propensity among the socialists than among, say, the capitalists to 'devote themselves to those intellectual pursuits which in modern society give them a decisive influence on public opinion'.

Should those concerned with the intellectual climate in which business operates be concerned about these scribblers of novels? How should they respond?

The power of fiction to convey a message is beyond question. As Hayek wrote *The Intellectuals and Socialism*, the British Broadcasting Corporation (BBC) was busy establishing a daily fifteen-minute wireless soap opera set in the mythical country village of Ambridge. Its purpose then was to teach farmers good new agricultural techniques to get the most out of the land in highly rationed post-World War II Britain. Today it is more likely to feature a politically correct lesbian couple on an organic hobby farm wanting to adopt a baby than an ordinary land-owning farmer off to market.

Another BBC offering, the combined 38 episodes of *Yes, Minister*, and *Yes, Prime Minister* by Antony Jay and Jonathan Lynn, is not so much comedy as a series of deeply insightful, highly educational, powerful training movies which have completely altered the way a generation looks at its government. Jay and Lynn's programmes, which were recently voted ninth in a compilation of the 100 best TV shows for the British Film Institute, removed our blinkers.

In the US, commentators from John Chamberlain onwards ('The Businessman in Fiction', *Fortune*, November 1948, pp. 134–48) have credited 'to some extent' the passage of the 1906 Pure Food and Drug Act directly to Upton Sinclair's depiction of the slaughterhouses of Chicago in *The Jungle*. Chamberlain wondered why, in the face of the incredible impact of his novels, Upton Sinclair continued to write as if nothing had changed, either on the part of the businessman or on the part of the legislators.

Surely the answer is very simple and has close parallels with the so-called 'environment movement' of today. Neither Sinclair nor the leaders of today's 'environment movement' is at all, not remotely, interested in improvement. The idea of a new, improved, kinder, gentler capitalism is utterly alien to them. They want to tear it down and destroy it: the novel or the 'environment movement' is simply a means to an end, the outright destruction of business, the total demise of capitalism.

In both cases – the novelist and the environmentalist – appeasement has never and will never work. Legislation directly addressing Upton Sinclair's worries did not slow him down one jot in the opening decades of the twentieth century and likewise with the environmentalists in the closing decades.

So how would I reply to the businessman who says, 'Look, John, we are getting a real bad press here with these writers of fiction. It isn't funny and over the long haul it is damaging our ability to provide our customers with quality products at a good price while simultaneously paying a good return to the pension funds who own us. What should we do?'

First, I would urge patience and caution. Three centuries of bad press will not be fixed overnight, and throwing millions of pounds at problems such as this by, say, endowing an Oxbridge Chair of Literary Capitalism is not only futile but also self defeating, as such resources will immediately be captured by the anti-capitalists.

Second, I would say that education is important and I would start a very modest programme of outreach to brand new emerging talent. A day spent visiting a factory or similar capitalist institution would be a positive eye-opener for most, if not all, such talent.

Third, my still modest outreach programme would extend to current leaders, both market-place practitioners and academic theorists, to engage them in whatever way possible.

Lastly, I would argue that incentives do matter, and I would seek to find ways of financially rewarding fiction writers above all who treat business as an honourable, creative, moral and personally satisfying way of life. Some of the pounds spent on appeasing might be better spent on encouraging and rewarding.

Finally a word about the origins of this book. They go back some years now to a series of conversations I had with Fiona Davis, then a policy analyst with the Confederation of British Industry (CBI). Fiona was a regular attender at IEA events and had a degree in English literature from Oxford University. My knowledge of the American literature in this area mentioned above but also including *The Capitalist as Hero in the American Novel* by John ('Jack') R. Cashill (unpublished PhD thesis, Purdue University, August 1982; printed by University Microfilms International, Ann Arbor,

Michigan, USA, 1985) led us to discuss the idea of an IEA publication on how business has been treated over the centuries in English literature. Pressures from other commitments stalled Fiona's progress, but serendipitously a favourable reference to Mrs Gaskell's *North and South* in an American magazine brought the name of Professor Arthur Pollard to mind and he caught the baton just in time.

10 FOREWORD TO *A CONVERSATION WITH HARRIS AND SELDON*

(IEA, Occasional Paper 116, May 2001)

Over the fireplace in the boardroom at 2 Lord North Street, the very room in which this conversation takes place, hang four framed photographic portraits. Top left is 1974 Nobel Laureate F. A. Hayek and top right is the entrepreneur Antony G. A. Fisher. Below Hayek is his pupil Arthur Seldon and below Fisher is his protégé Ralph Harris. This arrangement is quite deliberate and many is the time in that room when, speaking about the IEA, I have, pointing up to all four great men and moving my finger clockwise from Hayek, said: 'Hayek advises Fisher; Fisher recruits Harris; Harris meets Seldon. In nine words, that is the start of the IEA.'

So Harris and Seldon, armed with Hayek's little blueprint *The Intellectuals and Socialism* and funded (to a small extent) and encouraged in his capacity as Chairman by Fisher, set out to replace the prevailing big government/government-is-always-right orthodoxy with a more realistic and humane market-guided vision.

Did they succeed? It is an interesting and methodologically challenging question addressed elsewhere in *The Changing Fortunes of Economic Liberalism* by David Henderson.[1]

At one level they clearly did. When I first attended IEA events

---

1   David Henderson, *The Changing Fortunes of Economic Liberalism: Yesterday, Today and Tomorrow*, London, Institute of Economic Affairs, 1998

in the 1970s its three targets were inflation, the trade unions and the nationalised industries.

Inflation in the UK has come down from all but 30 per cent p.a. to about 2.5 per cent; trade union membership has dropped from just over 50 per cent of the workforce to just under 20 per cent (and nearly 30 per cent of union members now own shares, a higher percentage than the adult population as a whole); and the once hugely subsidised nationalised industries have become for the most part world-class tax-generating entities.

At another level though, one might ask, if socialism is dead, why is government bigger? If we share Mr Blair's new-found faith in a 'dynamic market economy' why does 'tax freedom day' advance rather than retreat? Why do spending and the clamour for ever more spending grow? Why do we set new records every year for regulation?

Ralph Harris often says that in the 1950s talk of markets was akin to swearing in church (particularly when applied to labour markets), yet by 1997 the word 'socialism' did not appear in the Labour manifesto. Is James Buchanan correct when he states 'socialism is dead but Leviathan lives on'? Is Ed Feulner on to something when he asks 'Can you win the war of ideas but fail to change policy?' Trust of government surely has changed during the years that unfold in this conversation. In 1964, Feulner reports, 75 per cent trusted big government. By 1998, exactly a generation later, 75 per cent did *not* trust big government. Is the Iron Triangle of bureaucrats, politicians and interest groups unbreakable or am I being too impatient as it rusts?

While it is hard to agree on the exact scale of change – and, as the dragons of inflation, trade unionism and nationalism were slain, so those of regulation, environmentalism and others promptly emerged – we can surely agree that the market approach is today in better shape than fifty years ago and that our two conversationalists, Harris and Seldon, were key movers and shakers in the process.

Having agreed that something of significance certainly happened, the interesting question then is how did it come about? What can we learn from the experiences of these two men so that they may guide us in this new century as we face new challenges? I list below the twelve most important lessons I learned from Ralph and Arthur in this 'conversation' and I urge you not only to read the full text closely but also to savour the commentaries which follow from a group of very distinguished thinkers from the UK and around the world.

1 Packaging your message

Because both Harris and Seldon sprang from working-class roots, they did not share the then common belief that such people 'could not do all the necessary things' (AS) to provide for themselves and improve their lot. This 'armed [them] against undue sentimentality' (RH), but it did mean 'it took us ten or fifteen years to make a mark because we started off appearing to be insensitive to the lowly' (AS).

2 Public choice and history: a blend

'They [the politicians] forgot all the history of the working classes' (AS). This is the very Hayekian point about the importance of history. It is the nationalisation of health and education and welfare (AS). It is the imposition of 'a common standard', compulsory rather than voluntary contributions 'and let the politicians for electoral purposes determine the benefits' (RH). It is the evil of public choice economics when political government replaced and destroyed individual and family choice (AS).

3 Inflation

'Inflation [is] the enemy of self provision' (RH) and in turn allows the government in to take over supposedly failed private provision.

4 Product development

Determining 'what kind of book is useful' (RH), 'a reading list' with 'footnotes to encourage the students to pursue the matters discussed in more detail' plus 'lively' presentation, accessibility and 'a good read' of 'about ten thousand words' (AS).

5 Patience

It 'took us five or ten years to win the confidence of some respected journalists' (AS).

6 Popularise

'Both of us were able to popularise, write in simple language, simple English, the arguments of our authors' (AS). 'No jargon or complexities to keep the everyday reader at bay' (RH).

7 Challenging scholars

A challenge to scholars: 'Stick to your last and tell us what you think your reasoning leads to' (AS).

8 Politically impossible

'We refused to limit ourselves to what government said they could do without risking votes and all that sort of stuff'(AS).

9 Shock tactics

'A lot of our thinking was deliberately intended to affront [the establishment] and wake them up' (RH).

10 Secrets of success

Three ingredients for success: 'academic something, business something and finance' (RH). Plus 'we had faith that knowledge would work' (AS).

11 Living with yourself

'If you feel you are right, you go on arguing until you are established as having told the truth. You can't live with the untruth if you feel you have found the truth' (AS).

12 Independence

Seeing people, great public figures in the House of Lords, not free to say what they want and voting even against things they actually believe in bring to 'my mind this enormous gratitude to have had what Antony Fisher called "an independent station"' (RH).

11 JUST IN TIME: INSIDE THE THATCHER REVOLUTION

(*Economic Affairs*, Vol. 21, No. 2, June 2000:
review of *Just in Time: Inside the Thatcher Revolution*,
by John Hoskyns, London, Aurum Press, 2000)

Speaking recently at the IEA at a lunch to celebrate the publication of *Just in Time* the author, Sir John Hoskyns, commented that we have to remember that people under 35 do not remember what the economic landscape was like prior to 1979. I intervened and said his figure should be more like 40, and even that assumed politically and economically alert 19-year-olds.

The starting point of this highly detailed and very valuable memoir is the appalling state of the British economy in the 1970s. And it is worth recalling how truly bad it was. Grotesque marginal tax rates; extraordinary meddling; rocketing numbers of civil servants; subsidies to nationalised industries going through the roof, 29 per cent inflation; rampant trade unionism and so on. The Germans likened the UK economy to that of East Germany; the French crowed over the '*dégringolade*' of our economy; and the world over it was called 'the British disease'. Britain was fast becoming the first fourth-world country, namely a rich nation returning to poverty.

It was truly pitiful, astonishingly so, and it is important that new generations are constantly reminded of the deep mire from which the UK economy emerged in the 1980s and 1990s. If the German psyche is scarred by hyper-inflation the British should be by hyper-degringolation.

Even more astonishing was the prevailing view that it would never ever get better. From Whitehall and Westminster via academia and the media to those twin pillars of the crumbling citadel, the TUC and CBI, a sense of irreversible decline dominated, monopolised even, the climate of opinion. An extreme variant of this view was that Germany and Japan were 'lucky'. They had been bombed and forced to start afresh with everything new. As I heard Hayek wryly comment: 'I do not think the solution to the problems facing the UK economy is to destroy all its fixed capital!'

This book is the memoir of the man who ran Margaret Thatcher's Policy Unit in 10 Downing Street from 1979 to 1982 and before that, after a career in the army and the fledgling software business, for two years (1977–9) worked for Geoffrey Howe, Jim Prior, Keith Joseph, Angus Maude and John Biffen, 'the brains of the party', on 'a coherent plan to lay ground, campaign and then govern'.

Interestingly for IEA subscribers the book twice credits the Institute as a foundation stone. In the Introduction (pp. xi–xiii) we read:

> The free market counter-revolution had been slowly gathering strength since the publication of Hayek's *The Road to Serfdom* in 1944, the formation of the Mont Pélerin Society a few years later, and the setting up of the Institute of Economic Affairs in the mid-1950s. I came late to all these exciting and then unfashionable ideas, but by the early 1970s I was reading most of the relevant books and also the IEA publications.

And in the Epilogue (p. 392):

'. . . Margaret Thatcher and her colleagues were the
beneficiaries of changes in economic thinking, coming from
the Chicago School and the IEA . . .'

Just how out of fashion such ideas still were in the mid and late
1970s is illustrated many times. Two of my favourites are his
sketch of Alfred Sherman whose devotion to markets was 'regarded in polite circles as eccentric or worse' and the story of
Hoskyns's first unpublished book. It was rejected. 'One [literary
agent] said that the book contained too many references to papers
prepared by the Institute of Economic Affairs, at that time regarded as out of touch with the realities of a modern economy.'

The book easily captures the feeling in the air that the UK had
become a stumbling, marginalised economy and that the forthcoming election was a last or, at best, next to last chance to do
something. But despite Hoskyns's constant references to the
chances of success being slim he still just fails to capture how low
expectations were. After all, the previous Tory government under
Edward Heath had been the most socialist of the century and the
cast had not changed much at all: Thatcher, Joseph, Howe – the
trio photographed on the cover – had all been senior Heath
cabinet colleagues who, as he often enjoys pointing out, had not
spoken out against his U-turns, and indeed had demanded more
and more resources for their departments.

So low were expectations of reform – Heath had privatised
Thomas Cook's travel agency and ten pubs in Carlisle – that, on
the Saturday after Geoffrey Howe's brilliant abolition of exchange
controls, a colleague commented to me at a conference at the
Imperial Hotel, Russell Square, in all seriousness that 'if we get
nothing else from the Tories than this it will still be a better

government than Heath's and this was far more than any of us dared hope for.'

The book is not an easy read but it is a valuable one. It is a guide book, an inside account of a five- to six-year period in which the foundations for later change and reform were laid. It is a pity it was not published four years ago. Its lessons are few but crucially important. *First*, the clear structure of production in the generation of ideas shines through from start to finish. There is the artillery (the IEA, Chicago *et al.*) and then there is the infantry (the CPS, the study groups, the committees and so on).The work of the artillery uncovered a set of principles, a compass to guide the infantry toward the targets it would have to attack. But it provided also a set of principles that would help in the day-to-day business of government. Mr Blair, on the other hand, got elected first, then waited a year and finally called a 'wonkathon'[1] one afternoon at No. 10 to find out what he should be thinking/doing. Naturally it got a lot of publicity.

Second, there is the selection of a small number of key issues – the unions, inflation and the nationalised industries – as being the essential prime focus for all available brainpower and firepower. The contrast with the Blair approach with its more than 100 review groups could not be more marked.

Third, there is the thinking that went on in opposition, knowing full well that once in government the civil service would make sure there was no time for something so dangerous as thinking, let alone thinking the unthinkable. Combined with this is Hoskyns's own repeated attempts not to get drawn away from his role as adviser rather than aide. The former is free to think and paid to do so;

---

1   A meeting of policy 'wonks'.

the latter is there to write speeches and pour drinks. The PPS to the PM must be the highest-paid barman in the world.

Fourth, there is the careful selling of strategy and ideas within the senior ranks of the Tory party. Eschewing big presentations to the entire shadow cabinet, Hoskyns and his team meet one on one with the Howes and the Josephs and rarely with more than three or four people at a time. One is struck by the quality of the talent then at senior level or just emerging and how economically literate so many were. There are the odd characters who fail to contribute much to the Hoskyns story (John Gummer and Chris Patten) and even some who are against: 'Ian Gilmour and Tim Raison wage a war of total inertia.' But with the Lawsons and Lamonts at middle management and the Lilleys, Portillos and Redwoods as junior officers some impressive minds were at work. Again the contrast with what Mr Blair has available to him could not be more stark.

Even with such brainpower as, say, Margaret Thatcher (chemistry and law) some hilarious insights emerge (p. 52):

> Our initial difficulties with Lord Thorneycroft stemmed from his inability to understand what we were saying . . . He frequently seemed to think that our . . . reports were draft speeches, public words rather than strategic thoughts. We sometimes had the same difficulty with Mrs Thatcher. Politicians seem to be more accustomed to being given words to say than thoughts to consider. Speeches are part of their everyday lives. Sustained, hard thinking about policy is often less familiar. When they are given ideas, they mistake them for speeches; and, too often, when they make speeches, they believe them to be a substitute for ideas.

Part of that last sentence deserves to feature in the Oxford *Dictionary of Political Quotations*.

Was Margaret Thatcher really not 'familiar' with 'sustained, hard thinking about policy'? Is the structure of production of ideas such that a political leader does not in fact think hard about policy? I doubt if Sir John is implying anything more than that 'she got the big picture, she sold it and she left the details to others.' If he is saying more, it would be interesting to feature his reply here in our pages.

Fifth, there is the careful orchestration of set speeches such that a Whitelaw statement linking major speeches by Prior and Howe on the union issue leads to significant and respectful press coverage: 'The press seemed to sense that an adult debate was at last beginning about a subject that worried many people.' Hoskyns is nothing if not a detail man. He recounts that on being introduced to the No. 10 staff he finds one to be 'distinctly guarded' and another 'scarcely able to conceal his hostility' (p. 98). Faced with this he takes many small steps to ensure he is not sidelined. He ensures his group is always called the Prime Minister's Policy Unit: not 'Number Ten' or 'Downing Street,' but 'Prime Minister's.' And while convention dictates his rank necessitates his addressing ministers formally, he addresses all bar the PM by their first name. And above all he makes his stuff interesting to read such that ministers hunt it out and make sure they do digest it.

To sum up, foundations lead to principle which gives you a compass; select a few targets; plan ahead; recruit; sell; orchestrate and pay attention to detail. It is almost military but then it is a war of ideas and this is an account of a battle written by a colonel. It is not so much a page turner, rather it's a must-read, must-digest mandatory how-to text for all who want to understand and influence change. And who knows, maybe there is a politician out there able to tell the difference between 'thoughts to consider' and 'words to say' and who does not find 'sustained, hard thinking about policy' alien. And if her ear were turned my way I would say: 'Look. Then it was the unions, inflation and the nationalised industries. Today it is the EU, regulation and the big spenders: health/education/welfare.'

12 THE HOOVER INSTITUTION

(*Economic Affairs*, Vol. 22, No. 1, March 2002:
review of *The Competition of Ideas: How My
Colleagues and I Built the Hoover Institution*, by
W. Glenn Campbell, Illinois, Jameson Books,
Inc., 2001)

It is hard to convey the importance of the Hoover Institution,
its sheer size, its growth under Glenn Campbell and its influence.
In 1992 *The Economist* rated it number one think-tank in the world
and that is hard to challenge.

In his book on President Reagan, Martin Anderson wrote of
Hoover leader Glenn Campbell, 'he is without peer, the premier
intellectual entrepreneur of this century.' And from Thomas Sow-
ell we learn that Campbell 'made the Hoover Institution the
world's leading refuge for ideas that were in danger of being
stamped out by academic intolerance throughout the Western intellectual world.' And Theodore H. White, in *America in Search of
Itself: The Making of the President 1956–80*, comments how Martin
Anderson's first policy paper for Governor Reagan in 1979 when
on leave from Hoover 'was a montage of minority ideas' which two
years later 'had become the law of the land'.

Such has been the success of Hoover under the author that you
could fill a large book full of plaudits, many of them from perhaps
surprising sources such as the left-leaning *New York Times* or
Marxist Sidney Hook.

Its archive tripled and became the largest private repository of
its kind in the world; its library added a million volumes; its fac-

ulty grew from a handful to over 100; its Press went from one or two books a year to 20 to 30; its scholars, led by Solzhenitsyn, Teller, Friedman and Hayek, won dozens of top awards; and its National Peace and Public Affairs Fellows Program has turned out to be a hothouse of new talent.

So it is a magnificent story of achievement, made even more magnificent by its setting in the extraordinarily difficult circumstances of a major university lurching to the left. I lived within a mile or two of Hoover during many of the episodes retold in Chapter 7, which is correctly called "The (Almost) Golden Eighties'. The struggles over ideology, free speech, Reaganite connections, fundraising, assets and governance were constantly on TV and made front-page news. Indeed when Leonard Liggio, Walter Grinder and I moved the Institute for Humane Studies (IHS) from Menlo Park, CA, to join George Mason University (GMU) in Fairfax, VA, the legal document drawn up by IHS for discussion with GMU's President Johnson was hugely influenced by the Hoover episodes we had witnessed down the road in Palo Alto. The use of 'at' was quite deliberate in the Institute for Humane Studies at George Mason University. Not 'of' or 'in' or a comma, but 'at' as in 'we could easily be "at" some other place if it did not work out'.

Unfortunately this book fails on several levels. While it is packed with endless data and dozens of documents, and the author takes on some issues, it is a missed opportunity. The sub-title is *How My Colleagues and I Built the Hoover Institution*. Yet in 400-plus pages I marked only two spots which I wanted to photocopy to colleagues.

The first (p. 43) comes from Campbell's days as Vice President of the American Enterprise Institute (AEA) in Washington, DC. Then called the American Enterprise Association, this was the job from which he was headhunted to California. Here he tells us how he learned 'that if innovative and useful policy-oriented research was to be done by eminent scholars, I would have to work *for* [his emphasis] those scholars, not attempt to direct their activity'. Later: 'I knew if I selected good, self-starter scholars, close supervision would not be necessary.' And pages 223 to 227 provide only some insight into his fundraising strategies when he clearly has a whole series of master classes bottled up in him.

For me the real story, the real value and insight that this book does have (and in spades) is what George Nash, President Hoover's official biographer, calls (p. 147) 'an inevitable *structural* tension' (his emphasis) of having an independent institution located within the framework of a university. This is the fascination from a non-profit management perspective of this 30-year battle between the overarching university and this 'independent' institute.

On page 66, Campbell accepts the job because the former President wants him; it is a chance to build; he is guaranteed first-class air travel; and he'll always be able to keep his special parking place by the Hoover Tower. As a young dad with two girls and soon a third he is also told at interview that the schools in Palo Alto are so good he will not have to pay for private ones! We are not told along which route he finally went in educating Barbara, Diane and Nancy.

First-class travel is clearly important to Campbell. Earlier (p. 62), while still at AEA, he travels to Europe on HMS [*sic*] *Queen Elizabeth* 'second class because we were returning first class on a new ship – the USS *United States* – and we wanted to save money for the American Enterprise Association, which was paying for the trip'. Campbell and wife were *en route* to the Mont Pélerin Society meeting in England and this story brings back a memory. *En route* alone to MPS in Mexico in 1990 I boarded my plane in Florida, walking through business class where many think-tank heads were sitting. I sat in the front row of economy with lots of leg room and five minutes later billionaire financier John Templeton joined me. People in business class are typically spending other people's money. People in economy are more likely to be paying their own way, and I've raised a lot of money that way.

Campbell walks into Hoover knowing of the problems. Indeed (p. 64) on his interview trip he writes of 'the stuffy, hostile atmosphere of Stanford'. And later (p. 135) on joining a faculty committee he 'immediately felt like a skunk at a lawn party'.

As the three decades unfold, so the problem worsens as Stanford moves left and Hoover goes in the opposite direction: 'Hoover is the only major think-tank that has managed to turn from a left-wing organization into a well-balanced and scholarly one that fosters a true competition in ideas' (p. 70). And as Hoover's income, endowment, library, archives and physical plant soar ever upward so, 'I was always on guard against the possibility that the institution would be targeted as a "takeover candidate" by certain avaricious Stanford professors and administrators. In this, the University did not disappoint me' (p. 219). Right at the start (p. 74) Stanford's President addresses an openly hostile Academic Council. He attempts to assure them that President Hoover 'could not live much longer and that things would then change to their liking'. Well, he clearly underestimated Campbell's tenacity and also Hoover's care in laying out the details of this unique arrangement (pages 76 to 80).

As Campbell tells his story my sympathies shifted back and forth. Yes, he was a staggeringly successful intellectual

entrepreneur. But he was running a programme within a programme with scant regard for the overall mission of the university itself. Two episodes are very telling. On Friday, 23 October
1959 we learn from a nine-page extract of President Hoover's
Notes (pp. 53–61) that the President has breakfast with Stanford's President Sterling. Hoover finally gets around to dis-
cussing his own fundraising efforts and seems surprised that
Sterling has approached the Rockefeller and Ford Foundations
'to contribute to other University programs'. Surely it would have
been a major oversight – a sackable offence – had Sterling not
been doing just that! And later (p. 162) Campbell reports, 'we
were not supposed to approach a possible donor until he or she
had turned down several of Stanford's appeals for funds.' Not
supposed to, but you can be sure he did. And you can be sure
that that must have been very irritating for the University. There
are other tensions. President Hoover (p. 47) refuses to take advantage of a new Act to do with the upkeep of Presidential papers
that would have brought $100,000 per annum to the Institution.
Campbell later (p. 90) regrets that Hoover's papers are elsewhere
and notes that by 1996 they would have brought an annual Federal subsidy of $2 million. Unlike all other self-proclaimed classi-
cal liberal think-tank heads I know, Campbell is happy to accept
tax dollars and does so often.

Too often, though, Campbell gives us a glimpse of an interesting topic or insight but then veers away, failing to follow through
and give us the full analysis and the benefit of his experience. To
give one example: 'businessmen, even the most successful, are in
awe of professors' (p. 133). He tells us how he does not fully understand this but he also uses this knowledge to great effect as he
builds the Institution. But how? And on one particular issue where

surely the author has a lot to offer, namely how to build your Board, he writes not one word.

The late Antony Fisher, who founded the IEA and went on to help so many institutes to get launched, always insisted that the groups he worked with be completely independent of political parties and other vested interests. Like me, he lived, from 1970 to his death in 1988, not far from Hoover and definitely in its orbit. While his wish that his groups be independent predates that period it must have been something of a vindication for his strategy as he watched the seemingly endless bloody battle that is told as these pages unfold.

On finishing *The Competition of Ideas* I wrote to four colleagues thinking of putting a think-tank at a university. It could hardly have been more timely and I told them all to buy a copy. I just wish the book could have fulfilled its potential, in which case I would have been on the phone buying fifteen or twenty copies for IEA trustees and staff.

13 ON MILTON FRIEDMAN'S 90th BIRTHDAY WE STILL NEED HIS REMEDY

(*Daily Telegraph*, 30 July 2002)

Milton Friedman is 90 tomorrow. The world's leading exponent of the superiority of voluntary action over coercion has lived to see the momentum of socialism slow from a gallop to a crawl. Reversing it is the next job, he says. Most men entering their tenth decade slow down. If anything, he is getting feistier, saying there is no need to worry over the euro. It will dissolve within five to fifteen years.

This month, the Bank of England could boast inflation bobbing along at just above one per cent. Friedman would not be impressed. That is still too high. Friedman argues that inflation is always and everywhere a disease of money. It is not caused by trade unions, oil sheikhs or even the weather. The defeat of inflation around the world is Friedman's great gift.

There is still much to learn from him in Britain, and not just about economics. Friedman does not praise capitalism solely for its efficiency. He prefers to point out that markets are indispensable for liberty and choice.

If liberty is to be preserved, governments must be stopped from encroaching on voluntary activities, competitive markets are the customer's best friend; and, where goods have to be 'public', then the subsidy must go to the consumer, not to the producer. There is every indication, for example, that, if properly packaged school vouchers were introduced, they would be very popular.

Friedman has exorcised the assumption that the free market is for numskulls. Once it was axiomatic that anyone of sensibility or intelligence could not be on the right. Friedman's intelligence and genial argumentativeness made it respectable to dissent from the lurch to the Left.

He wrote of his own hero, the Chicago economist Frank Knight: 'He had an unfailing suspicion of authority and an unwillingness to bow to any authority but reason. This did not lead him into arrogance, rather a special sort of humility.' That captures Friedman very well.

He never ceased to give thanks to the East Coast sweatshops that gave his parents their first toe-hold in America. Born in Brooklyn to central European refugees, he had a jolly but austere childhood. He worked his way through degrees at Rutgers, Chicago and Columbia. His CV is an alarmingly long list of scholarly papers, interrupted in 1976 by the Nobel prize. There is a connecting thread: 'markets work and they allow human co-operation to function better than any alternative.' He became a household name soon after winning the Nobel, when his 1980 bestselling *Free to Choose* and accompanying television series brought him worldwide attention,

His *Theory of the Consumption Function* (1957), which undermined Keynesian notions of the determinants of consumption and saving, is regarded by some economists as his most fundamental contribution. He went on to criticise the simplistic notion of the 'Phillips Curve' which purported to show that governments could trade off inflation against unemployment. He argued against 'fiscal fine-tuning' and for a simple money supply growth rule for governments. His best-known scholarly work, *A Monetary History of the United States 1867–1960*, showed that the Great Depression was the result of poor monetary policy by the Federal Reserve Board.

His revival of the money equation MV=PT (Money Quantity times Velocity of Circulation equals Price Level times Transactions) is for me the social science equivalent of Einstein's $E=mc^2$. Years ago, trying to find the Friedmans' apartment in San Francisco, I knew I was in the right location when I spotted a car with the number plate MV PT.

The great secret of Friedman is his compassion. He wants to see poverty disappear, and schools and hospitals flourish. But the consumer has to have the power – not the producer groups. For himself, Friedman wanted a life of the mind. He has been spectacularly successful.

His intellectual adventures started in Chicago: 'I was exposed to a cosmopolitan and robust intellectual atmosphere of a kind I never dreamt existed. I have never recovered.' Many of his pupils would say the same about his seminars. Across the globe, his students climb the rungs of power and Friedman is admired as much in Prague or Santiago as in Washington, if not more so.

A fellow Nobel laureate, Gary Becker, recalls his first day in class with Friedman: 'I had been a very good student at Princeton. My first day in Friedman's class he raised a question. I answered. He said: "That's no answer – that's just rephrasing the question".' George Shultz, a former Secretary of State, recalls faculty lunches in Chicago thus: 'Somehow Milton managed to set the agenda of argument and there was a saying "Everyone loves to argue with Milton, particularly when he isn't there", because he is such a good arguer.'

Although he has advised many heads of state, he does not seek out officeholders. He has lobbied Congress only once and earlier this year he initially said 'no thanks' when President Bush invited him to lunch. He was persuaded to say yes, but prefers to capture the best young minds and engage their loyalty.

During Vietnam, Friedman opposed the draft; a coerced soldier is a losing soldier. Friedman served on the Commission on an All-Volunteer Force, created by Nixon in 1969. Initially its fifteen members were split one third pro-draft, one third against and one third undecided. Less than a year later, Friedman had all fifteen unanimous in telling Nixon to abolish the draft and it is for this that he is probably most respected in America. He is the father there of the all-volunteer army.

Friedman despairs of businessmen ever becoming exponents of the free market, as they rarely match the intellectuals of the Left. And he scoffs at the dozens of chairs in 'Free Enterprise Studies' endowed by well-meaning millionaires. They are routinely captured by opponents of markets.

But at least the intellectual horizon has changed. Thanks to Friedman, socialism is increasingly a matter for archaeologists.

14 THE ACHIEVEMENTS OF PETER BAUER

(IEA, Occasional Paper 128, September 2002)

The Milton Friedman Prize

On Thursday, 9 May 2002, Peter Bauer was due to be recognised at the 25th Anniversary Dinner of the Cato Institute in Washington, DC, as the first-ever winner of the $500,000 Milton Friedman Prize for Advancing Liberty.

Unfortunately, Peter passed away on 2 May. However, he had been planning to attend and had written his acceptance speech. In the circumstances John Blundell, a judge who had already been asked to speak on the selection of Peter, gave not only his own speech but also the acceptance. Both are reproduced below.

On the stage at the dinner with Blundell was 1976 Nobel Laureate in Economics Milton Friedman and the Glass Prize Sculpture. Peter's executors asked that, as he had no family, the sculpture and certificate (also read out by Blundell) be put on permanent display at the Cato Institute.

The achievements of Peter Bauer
John Blundell

I first met Peter Bauer in the fall of 1971 when I was a freshman at the London School of Economics. The tutor assigned to me was slightly to the left of the Labour Party, which made him a moderate man for that time and place. He suggested at our first meeting that I write a paper for him on a topic of my own choosing so he could begin to get the measure of me. I replied, 'Well, how about something on the Economics of Development and the Third World?' and he seemed very pleased. A week later I handed in a paper entitled 'Trade Not Aid'. 'Oh dear,' he said. 'I'd better give you to Peter Bauer.' Peter's first advice to me was 'Don't read Hayek or Mises until you are a graduate student. As an undergraduate they will only get you into trouble.' Well, Peter was spot-on. But he was too late ... and I'm still getting in trouble.

His second advice was to study history and I recall Elton's *The Practice of History* being thrust into my hands. Without history we cannot understand society. Without history we cannot value and we certainly cannot reclaim liberty.

Thirdly he opened the eyes of a very narrow economist to the importance of an interdisciplinary approach to understanding society and to promoting liberty. But as well as being a great scholar and tutor Peter was also a man of great physical and moral courage, as he showed during the deadly student riots of the late 1960s when he publicly and boldly and repeatedly stood by his principles. He refused to let the left tyrannise him. He refused to let the left cow him.

So why did we, the nine judges, select Peter Bauer?

It was Peter who, after years of study of private enterprise in Africa and Asia, proved that the poor are *held back* by central planning, *held back* by large-scale state investment and *held back* by foreign aid.

It was Peter who showed that the solutions proposed by all other development economists were not solutions at all – nor were they even neutral. Rather they were positively harmful.

It was Peter who in the scholarly literature changed how we see the world within his meticulous analysis of markets and migration, population and price controls, investment and so-called commodity stabilisation schemes.

It was Peter who cautioned us not to use a warm, fuzzy word like 'aid' but rather the more accurate 'government-to-government transfers'.

It was Peter who taught that aid is the process by which the *poor* in *rich* countries subsidise the *rich* in *poor* countries.

It was Peter who showed us that peasants in poor countries routinely invest in crops which do not bear fruit for six years! That is, the poor peasant takes a longer view than most politicians.

It was Peter who conjectured that aid politicised and corrupted recipient countries, drawing talent into government that would otherwise have remained in the productive private sector.

It was Peter who exposed how aid reinforced unsound domestic policies ... to say nothing of repression and the expulsion of productive minorities.

It was Peter who, with Hayek and Mises, prophesied that the Soviet Union could not survive in the long term.

It was Peter who pointed out that in the Third World the primary aim of governments is to stay in power – and aid fuels this.

It was Peter who instructed us not to use the loaded term 'inequalities' but rather 'differences'.

It was Peter who opened our eyes when he commented how strange it was that the birth of a calf represents an increase in GNP and the birth of a child represents a decrease.

It was Peter who convinced us all that aid does not go to the miserable creatures we see on our television screens but rather to their rulers or, should I say, oppressors.

Finally, it was Peter who by personal example showed that, however much you are mocked and execrated, however shell-shocked you may be, you must continue to pursue the truth. And remember that when Peter started 'all', I repeat 'all', other development economists favoured 'central planning as the *first* condition of progress'.

Alas, Peter is no longer with us in person. But his courage and his teachings remain as an imperishable example to us and to future generations.

Two years ago I made a video of Peter with the Liberty Fund of Indianapolis, Indiana, and my last question to him was, 'How will history judge you?' He replied, 'I will not have the standing of a Hayek but I think I shall be commended by some people for clarity and courage.'

Well, Peter, there are rather a lot of people here tonight to commend you, above all others, as the first winner of the Milton Friedman Prize for Advancing Liberty.

Had Peter been able to be with us, I would now be presenting to him his certificate. Let me read it to you. It says:

The Milton Friedman Prize for Advancing Liberty 2002
Peter Bauer
In recognition of his tireless and pioneering scholarly
contributions to understanding the role of property and free markets
in wealth creation, his demonstration of the negative effects on
poor nations of government-to-government transfers, and his
inspiring vision of a world of free and prosperous people.
Awarded this 9th day of May 2002

I spoke to Peter the day after he got the news of his prize, about a month ago now, and he'd already written his acceptance speech, which I will read in a moment. But I want to convey to you a feeling of how pleased he was. I think to win a prize from Cato, his favourite think tank, would have been very special to him, and to win a prize named after Milton Friedman would also have been very special. But to win *the* Milton Friedman prize from *the* Cato Institute was almost beyond belief for him. So let me just conclude by reading to you the sixty or seventy words he penned and planned to deliver this evening:

> I'm much gratified by the Milton Friedman Prize from the Cato Institute. Cato and Milton Friedman have influenced the climate of opinion by heroically defending and encouraging the principles of limited government, personal liberty and self-reliance. It is also important for me to add that Milton Friedman has been my mentor over many years. Cato as an institution and Milton Friedman as an individual scholar have genuine influence. Certainly, they've influenced me. I want to thank Cato and Milton Friedman.

15 BEYOND IDEOLOGY: TOWARDS THE DEMISE OF THE STATE AND THE COMING ERA OF CONSUMER POLITICS

(*Scotsman*, 17 March 2003)

It has been called the eighth wonder of the world or, in Einstein's case, the greatest invention in all of mathematics. More prosaically we call it the power of compound, and it and other trends are about to change our way of life.

In school (the third form, I recall) Mrs Schofield told us one day about the Rule of 70. It's very easy. If something grows at 1 per cent a year it will double in 70 years. But at 2 per cent it takes only half that time and at 3 per cent only one third that time, or 23.3 years.

Why is this important for public policy? Well at 3 per cent growth we double our wealth every 23.3 years; yes, 23.3 years. Given such growth, our wealth will double by 2026 and quadruple by 2050.

Second, the deregulated competitive skies of the past two plus decades and the virtually totally unregulated internet have done three things. They have opened our eyes to what is possible in terms of standards and service; they have dispelled many statist myths; and they have left no place to hide for those who would assure us that only governments can perform certain functions.

Third, we are all living a lot longer. Life expectancy doubled in the past 100 years. In the next 100 years it might double again. Certainly, reaching 100 will become the norm for those born today.

Over a 50-year period, the Queen sent out 100,000 birthday telegrams to centenarians. That quaint custom will cease. Too many of us will hit 100!

Just this past year we reached a milestone when there were inexorably more of us aged over 60 than under 16 for the first time ever in our history. The implications for work and pensions are just enormous. No more firemen retiring at 50 on a pension equal to 100 per cent of salary.

Fourth, just as we all know in our hearts that public sector standards are going to the dogs – and data not corrupted by rent-seeking bureaucrats proves this time and again – so the private sector just gets better and better. Continuous improvement is a must, or you just die in global competitive markets.

Fifth, the locus of political decision-making is moving very quickly. Devolution is a sham; smoke and mirrors. The real trend is away from Westminster, Whitehall and our political parties and towards, rushing towards, Brussels, the NGOs and the pressure groups.

Fifty years ago the Tory party had 2½ million members, the RSPB had 60,000 members, and voter turnout was in the 80 per cents. Today the Tory party is one tenth its former size, while the RSPB is 20 times bigger and voter turnout has dropped from the 80 per cents to the 50s. Fewer than one in four of us voted for Mr Blair, the lowest mandate any PM has ever had.

So what do these trends add up to?

I find myself agreeing with Mr Blair far too often than is good for his future. He was spot on, for example, to describe the 2001 General Election so simply and directly as 'an instruction to deliver'. Our wealth, the growing inability of politicians to hoodwink us, and our growing life expectancy all add up to the death of ideology. New Labour is more than happy to contract with the private sector to produce what the voters want. New Labour, in particular, recognises that results not ideology count increasingly.

We are moving beyond ideology to an era of consumer-driven politics, an era where consumers organised in large pressure groups (not parties) will achieve their goals from education and the environment to health and crime prevention. And given the inability of the state to do anything pretty much except tax and fight wars, this heralds a huge growth in the private provision of public services, albeit tax-financed for the moment.

The politician who survives in the coming decades will be the one who learns from the States, where it has long been known that the best way to get re-elected is to deliver, regardless of party ideology. If the streets are thought to be cleaner and safer than the day you got elected then you will be re-elected. It's that simple.

So contracting out, privatisation, PPP and PFI will all continue and will grow and will move into areas still thought to be sacrosanct. One day cities will have three employees: a CEO/Manager; a lawyer to oversee all contracts, and a shared secretary. Or maybe it will be two employees with the secretary coming from Office Angels.

The ghastly redistributive competition they call politics will change from promising subsidies to making sure services are delivered in the best possible way. Voter turnout and party membership will continue to plummet as pressure groups grow.

Pensions and work will be changed out of all recognition. Saving will be made compulsory for a period until we are all firmly in the habit. The FSB will squeal like a skewered piglet, but all employers will be forced to put 10 per cent of all salaries into individual retirement accounts owned by everyone over 16. Even casual workers aged, say, 18 at McDonalds will see 10 per cent go that way. They will also own it, watch it grow and become vested in capitalism. And faced with life expectancies of 100, 110, 120 years, watch for people to have many separate careers. Perhaps a dashing business career to age 55; a period teaching to 75; then something part time to 95, and finally the golden years on a pension 79 years in the making before your large number of descendants see you on your way.

Where the state continues to fail us, we will see the growth of opting out. As with the growth of private health, so look for the home-schooling movement to explode, particularly in inner cities where groups of parents will say goodbye to mediocrity and hello to excellence. This will be led by minority groups which will give the few remaining politically correct education officials conniptions.

Finally, we will wake up to the utter depravity and ghastliness of our foster care system – foster damage is more accurate. Every night 65,000 kids go to sleep looked after by the state, and HMG is about as good at looking after kids as it was at running an airline. Graduates of foster care are hundreds of times more likely to be on the streets, in jail, on drugs and on welfare. Not 5 per cent or 10 per cent more likely, but hundreds of times more likely.

Using a new breed of emerging non-profit groups that act more like for-profit companies, we will privatise the whole of foster care. The result of raising children in private homes will be a more than halving of the population of our prisons.

Massively rising expectations, greater knowledge, growing life expectancy, failing public enterprises, continuous improvement in the private sector, falling voter turnout, failing parties, growing pressure groups: these are all powerful trends, but together they add up to a monumental sea-change.

The politicians who embrace these changes and work with them will be the ones my great grandchildren will read about in modern history, say 50 years from now.

16 LOOKING BACK AT THE CONDENSED VERSION OF *THE ROAD TO SERFDOM* AFTER 60 YEARS

(*Economic Affairs*, Vol. 24, No. 1, March 2004; forthcoming)

Sixty years ago, on Friday, 10 March 1944, F. A. Hayek published his classic *The Road to Serfdom*, the book that ruined his reputation among economists but made him famous and changed the world.

Thirteen months later, in April 1945, *Reader's Digest* published a condensed version of the book. Several times in the 1970s and 1980s I heard Hayek say, 'I thought it impossible to edit *The Road to Serfdom* to just a few thousand words, so imagine my surprise and my delight when they did such a good job!' What a compliment to the skill of the then editors. And what a powerful message it was about the dangers of planning, the importance of economic freedom, the need to limit power and the centrality of property rights.

And of course it was that condensation that led the founder of the IEA, Antony Fisher, to Hayek and led him, at Hayek's advice, to set up the IEA rather than enter politics. Rarely can an item in a magazine have had such impact on the conduct of human affairs. Ten years later Fisher published the IEA's first book. Twenty years after that, IEA 'clones' began to appear, and today there is a network of one hundred such groups all around the world.

As the 60th anniversary of *The Road to Serfdom* approached I trawled the web for copies of that April 1945 edition of *Reader's Digest*, an idea inspired by the example of my colleague Brad Lips, vice president of the Atlas Economic Research Foundation, Fairfax, VA. I wanted to get a flavour for the setting. Who were the people who did this condensation? What articles appeared with it? What does this all tell us of the era?

I found four copies for varying amounts ranging from $2 to $10. Two were in excellent condition, one was OK and one was terrible. *Caveat emptor*!

Looking at the cover, three things leap out.

First, the editors thought that *The Road to Serfdom* was so important they put it at the front of the magazine with the headline: 'One of the most important books of our generation'. It was the first time the editors had put the condensed book at the front, rather than the back, of the magazine. Second, the articles that follow are all condensed from other publications. There's no going out and commissioning new material or doing interviews with so-called stars.

Third, they clearly believed in their motto of 'an article a day of enduring significance'. April has 30 days and yes, there are 30 articles. And they are of surprisingly high quality. Very solid stuff. No pap here!

Turning to the inside cover we learn that 1.5 million copies go every month to 'men and women in service' and that a separate department has had to be established to handle such 'military subscriptions'. Every working day a staff of 50 handled over 8,000 address changes by hand, removing metal plates from file trays, forging new ones and replacing them.

A bit of simple arithmetic makes that 2 million address

changes a year for 1.5 million military personnel. So on average each person in the services was moving once every nine months.

Founders DeWitt Wallace and Lila Acheson Wallace are listed as editors, and it is Vol. 46, No. 276 which I struggle to understand. Below their names are listed the ranks of senior editors (nine) and roving editors (nineteen), several of whom stand out as having surely helped or supported the Hayek condensation.

The first is Max Eastman, the former organiser of the Men's League for Women's Suffrage, former editor of *The Masses* and co-owner of *The Liberator*, friend of and agent for Leon Trotsky, and great Russian expert. He was later an associate of Bill Buckley, Russell Kirk, James Burnham, Frank Meyer and Whittaker Chambers. After finally renouncing socialism in 1941 he became a roving editor for *Reader's Digest* and among his many books was *Reflections on the Failure of Socialism*, published as early as 1955.

The second is Fulton Oursler, as in Fulton Oursler Sr – Fulton Oursler Jr did not join *Reader's Digest* until 1956, and retired in 1990. Oursler Jr was the Oursler who went to China with Nixon. Oursler Sr was the author of *The Greatest Story Ever Told*, the American best-selling popularisation of the Bible. He wrote scores of books, edited *Liberty Magazine*, and co-founded *True Crime*, but it was *The Greatest Story*, filmed in 1965 with Charlton Heston, Telly Savalas and many others, which proved to be his greatest success.

Then there is Paul Palmer (formerly with H. L. Mencken at the *American Mercury*) along with the Harvard-educated, English-accented, monocled, best-dressed man in America, William L. White. White was a prolific author, distinguished war correspondent, newspaper proprietor and editor, and the husband of New York socialite Katherine White, once described by John O'Hara as

America's most beautiful woman, as well as being a confidante of Clare Booth Luce and Bernard Baruch.

Finally Burt MacBride leaps out: he was the father of the famous American author, lawyer and politician Roger Lea MacBride. As a teenager, Roger met *Reader's Digest* author Rose Wilder Lane through his father Burt. Rose's mother Laura Ingalls Wilder had authored the children's *Little House* books and she became his 'adoptive' grandmother, introducing him to free-market ideas. Rose meanwhile was writing *The Discovery of Freedom: Man's Struggle Against Authority*.

From that early exposure to ideas, Roger MacBride went on to graduate from Harvard Law School; extend and bring to TV *Little House on the Prairie*; serve as a Republican in the Vermont State legislature; become in 1968 literary heir to Wilder Lane and thus *Little House*; get elected as a 1972 Republican member of the Electoral College; cast his vote for the Libertarian Party (LP) Hospers/Nathan ticket rather than Nixon; himself run for President in 1976 on the LP ticket financed, it is claimed, by *Little House* royalties; and finally return to the GOP to chair the Republican Liberty Caucus. His Electoral College vote for Tonie Nathan was the first ever cast for a woman and the first for a person of Jewish heritage. It was not Geraldine Ferraro and it was not Joe Lieberman, despite what the game shows claim!

That is just five out of a grand total of 53 editors of all stripes.

Moving along, on page 1 the great economist, journalist and author of *Economics in One Lesson*, Henry Hazlitt (whose review in *Newsweek* exactly a decade later of the very first IEA book, George Winder's *Toward the Free Convertibility of Sterling*, led to it selling out and convinced IEA founder Antony Fisher to hire Ralph Harris as the Institute's first employee), writes that Hayek:

'restates for our time the issue between liberty and authority'. He goes on:

> It is an arresting call to all well-intentioned planners and socialists, to all those who are sincere democrats and liberals at heart, to stop, look and listen.

The editors then move in with:

> Professor Hayek, with great power and rigor of reasoning, sounds a grim warning to Americans and Britons who look to the government to provide the way out of all our economic difficulties. He demonstrates that fascism and what the Germans correctly call National Socialism are the inevitable results of the increasing growth of state control and state power, of national 'planning' and of 'socialism'.

The introduction then finishes with a quotation from John Chamberlain's foreword to the US edition:

> This book is a warning cry in a time of hesitation. It says to us: Stop, look and listen. Its logic is incontestable, and it should have the widest possible audience.

Immediately following the nineteen-page condensation is a two-page condensation of a Ralph Robey *Newsweek* article, 'What is being planned for you', with an ominous banner: 'What becomes of the enterprise which has created a great nation, when this pro gram gets going?'

What follows is a dire warning that Washington, DC, is planning:

- an overall 'planning agency' to control the economy

- councils on which labour, management and government will be represented
- production quotas set by such councils for every industry to ensure 'full employment'
- government guarantees for companies against loss by buying up anything that cannot be sold on the open market
- a system of permits for all new market entrants
- the permanent fixing and control of prices
- the fixing of wages and an annual guaranteed wage
- to offset a possible deflationary gap such that at war's end 'workers are to receive as much for 40 hours as they now receive for 48 hours'; and finally
- 'an enormous program of Government expenditures and expansion of Government activities'.

This last bullet involves spending on:

> not only regional developments of the TVA type all over the country, but housing, education, airport construction, both transcontinental and local road building, wholesale extension and increase of benefits of social security, and so forth.

Well, there it all was in *Reader's Digest* in April 1945 ... and condensed from *Newsweek*.

There then follows a wonderfully rich paragraph which I quote in full:

> For example take this excerpt from the *Wall Street Journal*: 'Suppose a man wanted to open a new shoe factory. "If he's got a new product that's needed, and the facilities and materials can be spared, OK," say the planners. "But if the

market is well supplied and leather is scarce, we would suggest some other line of endeavor. If he insisted on going into a business which was not approved, that would be antisocial – in the same class as opium smuggling – and police powers would have to be used." '

Setting up a shoe factory is akin to drug smuggling!

Finally the piece ends with three paragraphs that could have inspired Ayn Rand to write *Atlas Shrugged*:

Yes, those who are making these plans know exactly what they are doing. And make no mistake about whether they are smart. They are as smart, and clever, and ruthless, and determined, as any group in this country.

One further point. Do not expect this program ever to be presented as a whole for consideration by Congress. It will be brought out part by part, each apparently designed merely to meet a particular problem of pressing proportions. And every part will be carefully labelled with an innocuous name and wrapped around and around with beautiful and innocent-sounding names especially prepared to cover up the real purpose and intent of the proposal.

So if you happen to be a believer in individual enterprise and freedom, watch for the component parts of this program. And don't be misled by someone's telling you that we are just taking a small step toward 'industrial democracy' or a 'planned economy'. Rather remember that this same program when it was in effect in Italy was known as 'Fascism'. And today in Germany it goes under the name of 'Nazism'.

A final comment on the condensed version of *The Road to Serfdom*. On page 5 there is a sidebar offering reprints. It begins rather breathlessly:

> Undoubtedly *Digest* readers will feel that this is one of the
> most important and significant articles in recent years.
> Many will desire extra copies. Newsstand supplies of
> *Reader's Digest* are soon exhausted, but . . .

One reprint is 5 cents post paid and including the envelope. Ten will cost you 35 cents and 100 will cost $2.50. I wonder how many were ordered.

Page 22 concludes the section with the following 'Additional Comments on *The Road to Serfdom*':

> Sometimes it happens that a small book flashes a long light
> of warning and of hope. Such a book is *The Road to Serfdom*
> – one of the great liberal statements of our times.
>
> > John Davenport in *Fortune*
>
> In writing which is forceful and thoughtful . . . Mr Hayek
> expresses the fear that the democracies are moving step by
> step in the same direction that Germany went. This book
> deserves wide and thoughtful reading.
>
> > *Chicago Sun*
>
> The reader will emerge refreshed as from a great intellectual
> adventure.
>
> > *New York Herald Tribune*
>
> Definitely, an important book. Nobody can read it without
> learning much to his advantage.
>
> > Howard Vincent O'Brien in *Chicago Daily News*
>
> A very important contribution to modern political thought.
> There is little doubt it will create a sensation in this country.
>
> > *Kansas City Star*

Sixty years on the rest of this issue of *Reader's Digest* tells us a great deal about the times in which *The Road to Serfdom* appeared.

The magazine is surprisingly familiar to the modern reader. There are lots of little sections like 'It pays to increase your word power' and a mix of the heroic and the educational, yet with a campaigning tone and a clear set of values. What strikes the economist in me is that $25 is offered for entries for 'Picturesque speech and patter' and $200 is offered for entries to 'Life in these United States'. Two hundred dollars was then equal to 6 weeks' work at 48 hours per week by a female wartime factory worker. Today the rates in the UK are £60, £125 and £200 depending on the section. Also there is a slightly cryptic sidebar regarding a $25,000 contest for Ideas for New Businesses, which has attracted 49,000 entries. No wonder! $25,000 then is close to $500,000 now. The sidebar bemoans the lack of paper – because of the war, presumably. Indeed rationing pervades. Chippewa Indians in North Michigan are burying their dead with their ration books – I assume they'll need them in their next life! And a child accuses his dad of siring a new baby . . . just to get the shoe coupon out of the new ration book!

And war dominates the 30 stories taking up at least one third, from the horrors of Japanese prison ships and underground German factories to the courage of those smuggling people across the European continent. Very black-and-white. Them evil. Us good.

Four articles of a broadly political economy nature caught my eye and are worth noting, two *en passant* and two in more detail.

In a delightful piece, 'Household servants are gone forever', Mrs Shelby Cullom Davis (Shelby later became a most generous supporter of market think tanks in the USA) warns that maids will be very scarce after the war and if you do manage to get one then she 'will have the social and economic status of a factory or office worker'. She concludes with the following wonderful lines:

> When Mildred and her friends come trooping from the
> factories, they're going to find a whole new deal awaiting
> them. But they won't be the only gainers. By putting
> housework on a business basis, we'll get more and better
> service crowded into fewer hours, we'll end the mutually
> degrading mistress–maid relationship and we'll find new
> privacy and a more intimate family life. In short, by freeing
> domestic workers from their old servitude, we shall free our
> homes as well.

And at the very back of the issue is the blueprint for *The Good Life*, the classic BBC comedy about a Mr Good who gives up his advertising job so he and his wife can live a life of self-sufficiency. In 'The have-more farm plan for city workers', the Robinsons leave their Manhattan apartment for two acres in Norwalk, CT, 'about an hour' from Mr Robinson's NYC office. He continues to work but on weekends and evenings turns his two acres into a 'little farm', producing

> all our milk and cream, some butter, all our eggs, about 120
> pounds of chicken a year, several hundred pounds of pork,
> bacon and ham, plus rabbit, lamb, goose, raspberries, and
> all but a few dollars' worth of fresh, canned and frozen
> vegetables, plus fertilizer for our garden and lawn.

Whether the tax man, food police and planners would let him do this today is another matter, particularly when he starts selling eggs in his office at 60 cents a dozen or trades with local farmers and neighbours on a barter basis.

This brings me to 'Can we break the building blockade?' by Robert Lasch, condensed from the *Atlantic Monthly*. The tag line sums it up beautifully: 'Must a great postwar housing program be hamstrung by restrictive and obsolete building codes kept in force by pressure groups?' It's superb. It's the economics of politics. On finding it, I felt like an archaeologist unearthing a great find. It's all there in the Chicago home building industry of the mid 1940s:

- unions and businesses with vested interests
- price fixing and blackballing of new entrants
- rationally ignorant citizens
- artificially high costs kept up in the fiction of health and safety
- innovations outlawed to protect jobs
- standards mandated to make work and
- prohibition on imports such as those of cut stone from neighbouring Indiana.

For example, take this paragraph:

Union glazers frequently refuse to install windows fully fabricated at the mill. Painters rule out the use of spray guns, or even the use of brushes exceeding a certain width. In New York, lathers refused to install metal lath and metal rods which were not cut and bent, at extra expense, on the job. When prefabricated pipe of fitted lengths was delivered to a job with threads already cut, Houston plumbers demanded the right to cut off the threads and rethread the pipe at the site.

And this in the great bastion of free enterprise! The US edition of *The Road to Serfdom* came out on Monday, 18 September 1944 and was reviewed the following Sunday in the *New York Times* by Henry Hazlitt. At the time Hazlitt was preparing his own bestseller, *Economics in One Lesson* (1946), and the story of the Houston plumbers is on page 50 in the first edition and page 52 in the second.

The second major story to catch my eye was 'The veteran betrayed' by Albert Q. Maisel and condensed from *Cosmopolitan*. The tag line asks: 'How long will the Veterans' Administration continue to give third-rate medical care to first-rate men?'

This is three to four years before the Labour Government of 1945–50 nationalised the British health sector. But what a lesson this could have been. The author, an expert on military medicine, claims that soldiers receive magnificent health care; he says it is 'the best that modern medicine can provide'. But once they cease being active soldiers and become veterans, then they fall into the clutches of the VA or Veterans' Administration. Now America takes its veterans seriously. There is even a position in the Cabinet for Veterans' Affairs! It takes them so seriously it gave them its own mini-NHS decades before the NHS. Seventy years ago it had 100 hospitals costing $250 million and an income of $106 million. Adjusted for inflation, that is capital of several billion dollars and an annual income of over one billion dollars. So what did these poor captives, unable to move, unable to shop around with the subsidy attached to them, get?

Well, it is stomach-turning:

- overcrowding
- over-worked doctors tied down by red tape
- incompetent doctors who cannot get hired anywhere else
- negligent nurses
- flophouse reject food and
- exploitative concessionaries.

Just to start with.

All in all, 'third-rate treatment of first-rate men'.

But how had it survived by then for a good two decades? The answer is as familiar as the problem itself – namely spin, and fixing the way the data is presented. Smoke and mirrors. Or, as the author writes, they published figures that while 'technically correct, are actually deceptive'. And what a scandal they were covering up: more died than were cured. It makes the UK's quasi-Albanian system look not that bad.

When it comes to a solution, however, our expert in military medicine is out of his depth, and about all he offers up is better management, a new broom at the top and hopefully a great doctor who is a brilliant administrator.

It was an issue of *Reader's Digest* that changed the world, and to this day the IEA sells large numbers of the condensed version of *The Road to Serfdom* every year. One US foundation, for example, mails one to every single newly elected politician in the USA. And how remarkable that the same issue should carry such a rich array of other relevant materials, particularly the eerie and unnerving piece on the dangers of a nationalised health system and the uncannily insightful piece on Chicago's builders.

I recently asked both Antony Fisher's eldest child Mark Fisher and F. A. Hayek's only son Laurence Hayek whether they knew where their father's copies of that issue of *Reader's Digest* were. Neither could say, but Mark assured me his dad's would be well-marked. Laurence Hayek, however, told a powerful story of his own regarding the copy he owns and displays from time to time with a host of other Hayek memorabilia, most recently at the 2002 General Meeting of the Mont Pélerin Society. F. A. Hayek, he said, had two younger brothers, Heinz, a professor of anatomy at Vienna, and Erich, a professor of chemistry at Innsbruck. Heinz was nominally a member of the Nazi Party simply to keep his job. At the end of World War II he was taken to a de-Nazification camp at Würzburg in the American sector. At his second or third interview, the officer in charge arrived with a copy of *Reader's Digest* (April 1945) in his hand. He sat opposite Heinz, pointed to the cover and asked 'Is this man any relation of yours?' Heinz was taken by surprise; I think we can assume he had not even heard of *The Road to Serfdom*. Holding the magazine and seeing the words 'F. A. Hayek' and 'University of London' he exclaims, 'Yes! That is my brother!'

'You are free to go,' says the officer. 'And keep the magazine,' he adds. On the death of Heinz in 1980, his widow Erica gave this very same copy, stamped 'American Library Würzburg', to Laurence Hayek.

CHRONOLOGY OF THE IEA[1]

April/May 1945   Antony Fisher reads a summary of F. A. Hayek's *The Road to Serfdom* in the front of the April issue of *Reader's Digest*

June/July 1945   Fisher talks to Hayek at the LSE. Hayek's advice: avoid politics and reach the intellectuals with reasoned argument – it will be their influence which will prevail.

1948   Fisher publishes *The Case for Freedom*

1949   Fisher meets Ralph Harris at East Grinstead

June 1955   Publication of *The Free Convertibility of Sterling* by George Winder. Fisher signs foreword as director of the IEA

November 1955   Original trust deed signed by Fisher, John Harding, and Oliver Smedley

June 1956   Harris comes from Scotland to discuss with Fisher the creation of the Institute

July 1956   Trustees confirm appointment of Harris as general director

---

1   This chronology first appeared in *The Emerging Consensus?*, IEA, 1981, ending with an entry for December 1980. It was adapted and brought up to date for the first edition of *Waging the War of Ideas* by John Blundell and Lisa MacLellan and was then brought up to date for the second edition by John Blundell and Melissa Davis.

January 1957	Harris begins work (part time) as general director at Austin Friars
February 1957	Harris and Seldon meet at 4 Dean's Yard, Westminster
1958	Seldon appointed as editorial adviser
January 1958	Publication of *Hire Purchase in a Free Society*. Second edition in July 1959 edited by Harris, Seldon and Margot Naylor. Third (rewritten) edition in February 1961
September 1958	Publication of *The City's Invisible Earnings* by W. M. Clarke
December 1958	Institute moves to basement in Hobart Place. Publication of *The Future of the Sterling System* by Paul Bareau
February 1959	Publication of *Advertising in a Free Society* by Harris and Seldon
April 1959	Michael Solly joins as research and editorial assistant on six-month trial
June 1959	Seldon appointed as part-time editorial director
September 1959	Fisher, Harris and Joan Culverwell help to organise the Oxford Conference of the Mont Pélerin Society
October 1959	*Survey of Large Companies*, by Harris and Solly, published
December 1959	Seldon proposes a series of papers for economists to explore the market approach to issues of the day: these eventually appear as the Hobart Papers, with 146 published by mid-2003
January 1960	Publication of *Not Unanimous – A Rival Verdict to Radcliffe's on Money*, edited by Seldon

February 1960   Publication of Hobart Paper 1 *(Resale Price Maintenance and Shoppers' Choice* by Basil Yamey)

May 1960   Publication of *Trade with Communist Countries* by Alec Nove and Desmond Donnelly

June 1960   Publication of *Saving in a Free Society* by Enoch Powell

February 1961   IEA moves to Eaton Square

July 1961   Seldon appointed full-time editorial director

April 1962   A financial crisis. Harris and Seldon down tools (pens) and concentrate on fund-raising for three months

1962   Harris proposes the Eaton Papers to analyse the economics of information. Nine were published between 1963 and 1966.

Seldon proposes periodic field studies based on comparative pricing of state and private welfare to reveal the universal fallacy of post-war 'price-less' opinion polling that claimed to have found that people would pay higher taxes for more state expenditure. (Four studies from 1963 to 1978, assembled in 1979 in *Over-Ruled on Welfare,* later vindicate the IEA findings that the demand for welfare varies with its price.)

September 1962   G. E. Blundell joins part-time as treasurer

March 1963   IEA incorporated as the Institute of Economic Affairs Limited, a private company limited by guarantee

April 1963   John B. Wood appointed trustee

November 1963   The first Occasional Paper, *The Intellectual and the Market Place,* by George Stigler, in the series

	edited by Seldon. (131 Occasional Papers were published by the end of 2003.)
May 1965	The first of twelve 'Key Discussion' books is published, intended for sixth-form teaching
January 1966	George Polanyi joins as non-resident, full-time researcher.
	Dinner to celebrate IEA's tenth year, attended by 150 academics, businessmen and writers; principal addresses by Professor John Jewkes, Sir Paul Chambers and Lord Robbins are reproduced in Occasional Paper 8, *Economics, Business and Government.*
	Solly proposes a series of Research Monographs; by end 2003, 57 have been published
1967	Harris becomes honorary secretary of the Mont Pélerin Society. He later organises the meeting at Aviemore in 1968 and the Adam Smith Double Centenary Meeting at St Andrews University in 1976
June 1967	The first IEA Readings are published. By end 2003, 58 have been published
1967–8	'Hobart lunches' gradually evolve into discussions addressed by a visiting economist and presided over by Harris
February 1968	The first of four Background Memoranda is published
December 1968	Harris and Seldon draft *The Urgency of an Independent University*, signed by 100 British scholars
January 1969	Publication of *Towards an Independent University* by H. S. Ferris – the paper which provided the

	intellectual foundation for the University of Buckingham
1969	Wood joins staff part-time
April 1969	Harris initiates the Wincott Foundation in memory of Harold Wincott, to sponsor annual lectures and prizes for economic journalists. By 2003, 32 Wincott Lectures have been published as Occasional Papers or as part of an IEA Readings
May 1969	IEA moves to Lord North Street
September 1970	First Wincott Memorial Lecture by Milton Friedman on 'The Counter-Revolution in Monetary Theory'
1970	Seldon proposes the Hobart Paperbacks to analyse the transition from ideas to policy. By end 2003, 31 have been published.
	Seldon's study of state pensions, *The Great Pensions Swindle*, is published by Tom Stacey publishers
July 1971	Wood appointed full-time with new title of deputy director
June 1972	The first one-day seminar for IEA subscribers in industry, government, schools and universities etc. The proceedings are published in IEA Readings
December 1972	Death of G. E. Blundell
1972	Wood establishes the first of several agencies for overseas distribution of IEA Papers
October 1974	IEA author F. A. Hayek receives Nobel Prize in economics

January 1976	Harris appointed honorary secretary of the Political Economy Club
February 1976	University College at Buckingham opens to students
October 1976	IEA author Milton Friedman receives Nobel Prize in economics
January 1977	*Not from benevolence . . .* , written by Harris and Seldon in six weeks (and prepared and produced by Solly in fourteen working days), is published to mark the IEA's twentieth anniversary
July 1977	*Twenty Years of Economic Dissent* published, containing messages from Milton Friedman, Armin Gutowski, Chiaki Nishiyama, George Stigler, Sergio Ricossa, Harry Johnson, B. R. Shenoy, Jacques Rueff and Gustavo Velasco and speeches by Antony Fisher, F. A. Hayek, Ralph Harris, S. R. Dennison and Sir Keith Joseph from the IEA anniversary dinner on 6 July 1977
1977	Seldon's study of pricing for 'public' services published as *Charge* by Temple Smith
1978	*The Coming Confrontation* published with a contribution by HRH The Duke of Edinburgh
June 1979	Harris raised to the peerage as Lord Harris of High Cross
mid–end 1980	IEA staff, in conversations, encourage Dr Digby Anderson to found an independent institute – The Social Affairs Unit – and assist him in finding financial support, with advice and 'house room'. The Unit is finally founded on

	receiving independent charitable status on 12 December 1980
July 1980	Harris proposes creation of the Patrick Hutber Memorial, a residence for students at the University College at Buckingham
August 1980	*The Times* publishes Seldon's 'predictions': 'China will go capitalist, Soviet Russia will not survive the century, Labour as we know it will never rule again.'
September 1980	Seldon appointed to board of the Mont Pélerin Society
October 1980	The first number of *The Journal of Economic Affairs* (quarterly) is published by Basil Blackwell, proposed and edited by Seldon
1980	Martin Wassell appointed editorial director to succeed Seldon. He works with Seldon until his first retirement in 1981
October 1982	IEA author George Stigler received Nobel Prize in economics
1982	Seldon nominated a vice-president of the Mont Pélerin Society.
1983	Seldon awarded CBE
June 1984	Hayek awarded the Companion of Honour
July 1984	Centre for Research into Communist Economies (CRCE) established as an independent organisation housed at the IEA. Fisher and Harris appointed as trustees, with Fisher serving as chairman of trustees
September 1984	The first CRCE publication, *Market or Plan* by Milton Friedman with a comment by Alec Nove

1985	Wood appointed editorial director
October 1986	IEA author James Buchanan receives Nobel Prize in economics
1986	Seldon re-appointed editorial director. Publication of *The Unfinished Agenda: Essays on the Political Economy of Government Policy in Honour of Arthur Seldon*. Health and Welfare Unit established; Dr David G. Green appointed director
January 1987	Graham Mather joins staff; he succeeds Harris as general director in September 1987
April 1987	Dinner held to mark IEA's 30th anniversary. Speeches by Antony Fisher, Sir Alastair Burnet, Sir Alan Peacock, Sir Keith Joseph, Lord Grimond, Lord Houghton, Samuel Brittan, John Horam, Lord Harris, Graham Mather and the Prime Minister, Margaret Thatcher
June 1988	Founder Antony Fisher knighted
July 1988	Death of Sir Antony Fisher; Lord Vinson LVO appointed chairman of the board. Nigel Lawson speaks at the IEA Special Lecture (which becomes the annual Hayek Memorial Lecture). His speech, *The State of the Market*, is printed as Occasional Paper 80
1988	Seldon retires as editorial director; Cento Veljanovski appointed editorial director
July 1989	Robin Leigh-Pemberton speaks at the IEA Special Lecture. His speech, *The Future of Monetary Arrangements in Europe*, is printed as Occasional Paper 82

December 1989	Harris retires from IEA staff
July 1990	Karl Otto Pohl speaks at the IEA Special Lecture. His speech, *Two Monetary Unions – the Bundesbank's View*, is printed as Readings 33
1990	Seldon's book *Capitalism* published by Blackwell. Hayek leaves a request in the manuscript of Volume III of *Law, Legislation and Liberty* that if ill-health prevents him from completing the book, he would like the task undertaken by Seldon
August 1991	Death of John B. Wood
October 1991	Ronald Coase receives Nobel Prize in economics
November 1991	Hayek awarded the Presidential Medal of Freedom by President George Bush, but is too frail to travel. His son, Dr Laurence Hayek, accepts it on his behalf
March 1992	Professor Colin Robinson appointed editorial director
April 1992	Graham Mather steps down as general director; Russell Lewis appointed acting general director
June 1992	Jeffrey Sachs (Harvard University) gives first Annual Hayek Memorial Lecture
October 1992	IEA friend Gary Becker receives Nobel Prize in economics
1992	Sir Antony Fisher International Memorial Award given to Seldon's *Capitalism*
January 1993	John Blundell takes up appointment as general director; talks with Roger Bate about setting up an Environment Unit

March 1993	Occasional Lecture series begins with Professor Richard Stroup
May 1993	*Families without Fatherhood by* Norman Dennis and George Erdos receives a Sir Antony Fisher International Memorial Award.
	First Annual John B. Wood International Memorial Essay Contest; prizes handed out to students by Blundell as chairman of the judges at May Hobart; brother Hugh Wood pledges a decade's support for the memorial
June 1993	Michael Novak (American Enterprise Institute) gives second Annual Hayek Memorial Lecture
September 1993	Christine Blundell launches IEA student outreach programme
October 1993	IEA and London Business School launch annual lecture series on utility regulation
November 1993	All conferences sub-contracted to two commercial firms. Library reconstructed and renamed The Arthur Seldon Room for Seldon's creation of the IEA's reputation for scholarship in defiance of 'political impossibility'
March 1994	Environment Unit formally launched at first annual conference, and publication of first Environment Unit book, *Global Warming: Apocalypse or Hot Air?*; sold out in six months – second impression needed by August
June 1994	Peter Sutherland (Director General, GATT) gives third Annual Hayek Memorial Lecture, published as *A New Framework for International Economic Relations*

September 1994   *Federalism and Free Trade* by Jean-Luc Migue receives a Sir Antony Fisher International Memorial Award

December 1994   Surprise publication of *No, Prime Minister!*, a collection of 30 essays by Harris, on the occasion of his 70th birthday

1994   Seldon's anthology (75 of 250 essay-articles, 1936–92) on the inevitably dwindling welfare state, published as *The State is Rolling Back* by the IEA/E&L Books

May 1995   Professor Harold Rose succeeds Lord Vinson as chairman of the board; Lord Vinson becomes vice president

June 1995   The Rt Hon. Francis Maude (Morgan Stanley International) gives the fourth Annual Hayek Memorial Lecture, published as *State and Society: Restoring the Balance*

1995   Blundell and Dr James Tooley discuss setting up the Education and Training Unit; it is formally launched in September

April 1996   Publication of first Education and Training Unit book, *Education Without the State* by Tooley

May 1996   *Global Warming: Apocalypse or Hot Air?* by Roger Bate and Julian Morris receives a Sir Antony Fisher International Memorial Award. Hobart lunch turns into surprise 80th birthday party for Seldon. Blundell gets more than 100 friends and colleagues (including 5 Nobel laureates) from 14 countries to send letters of tribute; these are later privately published with

	additional material by Marjorie Seldon in *Letters on a Birthday: The Unfinished Agenda of Arthur Seldon*
June 1996	Dr Donald Brash (Governor, Reserve Bank of New Zealand) gives fifth Annual Hayek Memorial Lecture; see December 1996 below
September 1996	Seldon appointed first-ever honorary fellow of the Mont Pélerin Society at Vienna meeting. IEA purchases freehold to 2 Lord North Street for £862,500
December 1996	Publication of Occasional Paper Number 100, *New Zealand's Remarkable Reforms*
1996	Seldon appointed consultant for external promotion of IEA scholarship. IEA turnover surpasses £1 million mark
February 1997	Gerald Frost, Deepak Lal and Brian Hindley move the Trade and Development Unit from the Centre for Policy Studies to the IEA. Occasional Discussion series begins with a programme on a market in airport landing slots
March 1997	*Economic Affairs* re-launched in new design, published by Blackwell, from Volume 17, no.1
April 1997	Harris and Seldon represent IEA at special meeting of the Mont Pélerin Society in Mont Pélerin. *Community Without Politics: A Market Approach to Welfare Reform* receives a Sir Antony Fisher International Memorial Award
June 1997	Dr Vaclav Klaus (Prime Minister of the Czech Republic) gives sixth Annual Hayek Memorial

	Lecture, 'The transformation of Czech society: retrospect and prospect', published in *Economic Affairs*
1998	State of the Economy conference moves to being held twice a year
May 1998	Sir Peter Walters appointed chairman of the managing trustees
September 1998	Blundell elected to the board of the Mont Pélerin Society
1998	Dr Jonathan Sacks (the Chief Rabbi) gives seventh Annual Hayek Memorial Lecture on the topic of 'Morals and markets', later published as Occasional Paper 108
March 1999	Arthur Seldon receives an honorary PhD from the University of Buckingham
May 1999	Professor Otmar Issing (member of the executive board of the European Central Bank) gives eighth Annual Hayek Memorial Lecture, published in March 2000 as *Hayek, Currency, Competition and European Monetary Union*
August 1999	Expansion of The Arthur Seldon Room
September 1999	Death of trustee Professor Michael Beesley. Annual Regulation Lecture Series becomes the Beesley Lectures in his honour
October 1999	Trustees challenge Dr David Green to make business plan for a new institute
June 2000	Blundell presented with Aims of Industry Free Enterprise Award by Sir Nigel Mobbs with remarks by Lord Forsyth and Mike Fisher.

	Dr Benno Schmidt (Edison Schools) gives ninth Annual Hayek Memorial Lecture
August 2000	Completion of launch of IEA Health & Welfare Unit as CIVITAS, The Institute for the Study of Civil Society: chairman, Lord Harris of High Cross
October 2000	Launch of *A Conversation with Lord Peter Bauer*, a Liberty fund video, with Bauer interviewed by Blundell
November 2000	London announced as the venue for the 2002 Mont Pélerin Society general meeting with Blundell as chairman of host committee
December 2000	Dr Arthur Seldon appointed honorary fellow of the LSE
February 2001	Publication of first IEA title in association with Profile Books
May 2001	Professor David Myddelton appointed chairman of the managing trustees.
	Dr Arthur Seldon's 85th birthday; *A Conversation with Harris & Seldon* (Occasional Paper 116) published to coincide with the event
July 2001	Charles Calomiris speaks on the topic of 'A globalist manifesto for public policy' at the tenth Annual Hayek Memorial Lecture, sponsored by Nomura. *A Globalist Manifesto for Public Policy* is later published as Occasional Paper 124
October 2001	Blundell presides at conference to mark the anniversary of the opening of the University of Buckingham and IEA publishes *Buckingham at 25*

November 2001   America's 'top cop' Ed Davis visits the IEA and
                 gives public lecture

December 2001   Sir John Templeton pledges $250,000 for three-
                 year expansion of outreach to students and
                 teachers

April 2002   Professor Patrick Minford and Carolyn
                 Fairbairn join the IEA board of trustees

May 2002   IEA takes over running of the National Free
                 Enterprise Award from Aims of Industry.
                 IEA author Peter Bauer posthumously receives
                 first Milton Friedman Prize for Advancing
                 Liberty from the Cato Institute. Blundell, a
                 judge, makes both the presentation and
                 acceptance speeches.
                 Launch of the Liberty Fund video *A Conversation
                 with Alan Walters* with Blundell as interviewer.
                 Kevin Bell and Professor Tim Congdon join the
                 IEA board of trustees

June 2002   Hernando de Soto speaks on the topic of 'The
                 road to capitalism and the spontaneous
                 generation of law' at the eleventh Annual Hayek
                 Memorial Lecture, sponsored by Nomura

July 2002   Professor Colin Robinson retires as editorial
                 director and addresses Hobart Lunch on the
                 theme of 'Markets, perfect and imperfect: 50
                 years on'.
                 IEA friend Milton Friedman turns 90. Blundell
                 writes lead op-ed in the *Daily Telegraph*: 'On
                 Friedman's 90th birthday we still need his
                 remedy'.

	The Making of the Institute, a selection of Arthur Seldon's prefaces (1960–92), is published as a hardback book
September 2002	Professor Philip Booth, Associate Dean of Sir John Cass Business School, commences duties as editorial and programme director
October 2002	Blundell hosts Mont Pélerin Society 2002 general meeting at the Queen Elizabeth II conference centre, attended by 545 delegates from 47 countries. During the event it is announced that IEA author and academic advisory council member Professor Vernon Smith has received the 2002 Nobel Prize in Economics
November 2002	National Free Enterprise Award, now run by the IEA, goes to Lloyd Dorfman, chief executive of Travelex
December 2002	Former IEA production manager Mike Solly dies
February 2003	IEA and Cass Business School launch annual lecture series on financial regulation
May 2003	Twentieth 'State of the Economy' conference held at RSA
June 2003	Bill Emmott, editor-in-chief at *The Economist*, speaks on the topic of 'Saving capitalism from itself' at the twelfth Annual Hayek Memorial Lecture, sponsored by Nomura
November 2003	Twenty-first 'State of the Economy' conference held at RSA. National Free Enterprise Award goes to Rodney Leach, director, Jardine Matheson Holdings

ABOUT THE IEA

The Institute is a research and educational charity (No. CC 235 351), limited by guarantee. Its mission is to improve understanding of the fundamental institutions of a free society with particular reference to the role of markets in solving economic and social problems.

The IEA achieves its mission by:

- a high quality publishing programme
- conferences, seminars, lectures and other events
- outreach to school and college students
- brokering media introductions and appearances

The IEA, which was established in 1955 by the late Sir Antony Fisher, is an educational charity, not a political organisation. It is independent of any political party or group and does not carry on activities intended to affect support for any political party or candidate in any election or referendum, or at any other time. It is financed by sales of publications, conference fees and voluntary donations.

In addition to its main series of publications the IEA also publishes a quarterly journal, *Economic Affairs*, and has two specialist programmes – Environment and Technology, and Education.

The IEA is aided in its work by a distinguished international Academic Advisory Council and an eminent panel of Honorary Fellows. Together with other academics, they review prospective IEA publications, their comments being passed on anonymously to authors. All IEA papers are therefore subject to the same rigorous independent refereeing process as used by leading academic journals.

IEA publications enjoy widespread classroom use and course adoptions in schools and universities. They are also sold throughout the world and often translated/reprinted.

Since 1974 the IEA has helped to create a world-wide network of 100 similar institutions in over 70 countries. They are all independent but share the IEA's mission.

Views expressed in the IEA's publications are those of the authors, not those of the Institute (which has no corporate view), its Managing Trustees, Academic Advisory Council members or senior staff.

Members of the Institute's Academic Advisory Council, Honorary Fellows, Trustees and Staff are listed on the following page.

The Institute gratefully acknowledges financial support for its publications programme and other work from a generous benefaction by the late Alec and Beryl Warren.

165

Other papers recently published by the IEA include:

WHO, What and Why?

Transnational Government, Legitimacy and the World Health Organization
Roger Scruton
Occasional Paper 113; ISBN 0 255 36487 3
£8.00

The World Turned Rightside Up

A New Trading Agenda for the Age of Globalisation
John C. Hulsman
Occasional Paper 114; ISBN 0 255 36495 4
£8.00

The Representation of Business in English Literature

Introduced and edited by Arthur Pollard
Readings 53; ISBN 0 255 36491 1
£12.00

Anti-Liberalism 2000

The Rise of New Millennium Collectivism
David Henderson
Occasional Paper 115; ISBN 0 255 36497 0
£7.50

Capitalism, Morality and Markets

Brian Griffiths, Robert A. Sirico, Norman Barry & Frank Field
Readings 54; ISBN 0 255 36496 2
£7.50

A Conversation with Harris and Seldon

Ralph Harris & Arthur Seldon
Occasional Paper 116; ISBN 0 255 36498 9
£7.50

Malaria and the DDT Story

Richard Tren & Roger Bate
Occasional Paper 117; ISBN 0 255 36499 7
£10.00

A Plea to Economists Who Favour Liberty: Assist the Everyman

Daniel B. Klein
Occasional Paper 118; ISBN 0 255 36501 2
£10.00

Waging the War of Ideas

John Blundell
Occasional Paper 119; ISBN 0 255 36500 4
£10.00

The Changing Fortunes of Economic Liberalism

Yesterday, Today and Tomorrow
David Henderson
Occasional Paper 105 (new edition); ISBN 0 255 36520 9
£12.50

The Global Education Industry

Lessons from Private Education in Developing Countries
James Tooley
Hobart Paper 141 (new edition); ISBN 0 255 36503 9
£12.50

Saving Our Streams

The Role of the Anglers' Conservation Association in
Protecting English and Welsh Rivers
Roger Bate
Research Monograph 53; ISBN 0 255 36494 6
£10.00

Better Off Out?

The Benefits or Costs of EU Membership
Brian Hindley & Martin Howe
Occasional Paper 99 (new edition); ISBN 0 255 36502 0
£10.00

Buckingham at 25

Freeing the Universities from State Control
Edited by James Tooley
Readings 55; ISBN 0 255 36512 8
£15.00

Lectures on Regulatory and Competition Policy

Irwin M. Stelzer
Occasional Paper 120; ISBN 0 255 36511 X
£12.50

Misguided Virtue

False Notions of Corporate Social Responsibility
David Henderson
Hobart Paper 142; ISBN 0 255 36510 1
£12.50

HIV and Aids in Schools

The Political Economy of Pressure Groups and Miseducation
Barrie Craven, Pauline Dixon, Gordon Stewart & James Tooley
Occasional Paper 121; ISBN 0 255 36522 5
£10.00

The Road to Serfdom

The Reader's Digest condensed version
Friedrich A. Hayek
Occasional Paper 122; ISBN 0 255 36530 6
£7.50

Bastiat's *The Law*

Introduction by Norman Barry
Occasional Paper 123; ISBN 0 255 36509 8
£7.50

A Globalist Manifesto for Public Policy

Charles Calomiris
Occasional Paper 124; ISBN 0 255 36525 X
£7.50

Euthanasia for Death Duties

Putting Inheritance Tax Out of Its Misery
Barry Bracewell-Milnes
Research Monograph 54; ISBN 0 255 36513 6
£10.00

Liberating the Land

The Case for Private Land-use Planning
Mark Pennington
Hobart Paper 143; ISBN 0 255 36508 x
£10.00

IEA Yearbook of Government Performance 2002/2003

Edited by Peter Warburton
Yearbook 1; ISBN 0 255 36532 2
£15.00

Britain's Relative Economic Performance, 1870–1999

Nicholas Crafts
Research Monograph 55; ISBN 0 255 36524 1
£10.00

Should We Have Faith in Central Banks?

Otmar Issing
Occasional Paper 125; ISBN 0 255 36528 4
£7.50

The Dilemma of Democracy

Arthur Seldon
Hobart Paper 136 (reissue); ISBN 0 255 36536 5
£10.00

Capital Controls: a 'Cure' Worse Than the Problem?

Forrest Capie
Research Monograph 56; ISBN 0 255 36506 3
£10.00

The Poverty of 'Development Economics'

Deepak Lal
Hobart Paper 144 (reissue); ISBN 0 255 36519 5
£15.00

Should Britain Join the Euro?

The Chancellor's Five Tests Examined
Patrick Minford
Occasional Paper 126; ISBN 0 255 36527 6
£7.50

Post Communist Transition: Some Lessons

Leszek Balcerowicz
Occasional Paper 127; ISBN 0 255 36533 0
£7.50

A Tribute to Peter Bauer

John Blundell et al.

Occasional Paper 128; ISBN 0 255 36531 4

£10.00

Employment Tribunals

Their Growth and the Case for Radical Reform

J. R. Shackleton

Hobart Paper 145; ISBN 0 255 36515 2

£10.00

Fifty Economic Fallacies Exposed

Geoffrey E. Wood

Occasional Paper 129; ISBN 0 255 36518 7

£12.50

A Market in Airport Slots

Keith Boyfield (editor), David Starkie, Tom Bass & Barry Humphreys

Readings 56; ISBN 0 255 36505 5

£10.00

Money, Inflation and the Constitutional Position of the Central Bank

Milton Friedman & Charles A. E. Goodhart

Readings 57; ISBN 0 255 36538 1

£10.00

railway.com

Parallels between the early British railways and the ICT revolution

Robert C. B. Miller

Research Monograph 57; ISBN 0 255 36534 9

£12.50

The Regulation of Financial Markets

Edited by Philip Booth & David Currie

Readings 58; ISBN 0 255 36551 9

£12.50

Climate Alarmism Reconsidered

Robert L. Bradley Jr

Hobart Paper 146; ISBN 0 255 36541 1

£12.50

Government Failure: E. G. West on Education

Edited by James Tooley & James Stanfield

Occasional Paper 130; ISBN 0 255 36552 7

£12.50

To order copies of currently available IEA papers, or to enquire about availability, please contact:

Lavis Marketing
IEA orders
FREEPOST lon21280
Oxford OX3 7BR

Tel: 01865 767575
Fax: 01865 750079
Email: orders@lavismarketing.co.uk

The IEA also offers a subscription service to its publications. For a single annual payment, currently £40.00 in the UK, you will receive every title the IEA publishes across the course of a year, invitations to events, and discounts on our extensive back catalogue. For more information, please contact:

Subscriptions
The Institute of Economic Affairs
2 Lord North Street
London SW1P 3LB

Tel: 020 7799 8900
Fax: 020 7799 2137
Website: www.iea.org.uk